OSCAR WILDE
AND HIS CIRCLE

Simon Callow

Published in Great Britain by National Portrait Gallery Publications,
National Portrait Gallery, St Martin's Place, London WC2H 0HE

ISBN 1 85514 312 7

A catalogue record for this book is available from the British Library

Publishing Manager: Jacky Colliss Harvey
Series Editor: Susie Foster
Project Editor: Celia Jones
Series Designer: Karen Stafford
Production: Ruth Müller-Wirth
Printed by EBS, Verona

Front cover
Oscar Wilde, 1854–1900
Elliott & Fry, 1881 (detail)
Modern print from a half-plate glass negative, 20.5 x 14.8cm
© National Portrait Gallery (x82203)

For a complete catalogue of current publications, please write to the
address above, or visit our website on www.npg.org.uk/pubs

CONTENTS

This book is dedicated with love to Patrick Garland,
co-worker, dear friend and informed Oscarian.

FOREWORD

I have been fascinated by Oscar Wilde since at least the age of twelve. The plays and the essays were the beginning of my self-education; like many others, I fell entirely under the spell of the man as revealed in Hesketh Pearson's trail-blazing *Life* and Rupert Hart-Davis's even more revealing edition of the *Letters* as intensely as if I had known him myself. I started to collect Wildeana; at the age of eighteen I wrote a play about him in fourteen scenes (after the fourteen Stations of the Cross, of course). At one point I could truthfully boast, as far as I know, that I had read everything on the subject in print in English. I could certainly not make that boast today; Wilde studies has become one of the great growth industries of the late twentieth century. The present volume makes no pretence to original research, but I hope that the format of the group portrait has enabled me to tell the great story from a variety of perspectives, so that Wilde is seen, as it were, walking through a Hall of Mirrors. There is a fine maquette for a sculpture of Wilde by Andrew Logan, made, like all of the sculptor's work, with shards of mirror. It is the perfect medium for a representation of Wilde, whose many aspects form a perfect reflection of the reader of his work, or the contemplator of his personality; if the present small volume were some kind of a verbal equivalent of Logan's Wilde, I should be very happy.

There is a complete list of sources at the back of the book, but no one who writes about Wilde can fail to plunder the great biography by Richard Ellmann, whose thoroughness, imagination and sympathy make it almost definitive, though Pearson's book perhaps remains indispensable as an evocation of the man in his time. Hart-Davis's great edition of the *Letters* was the turning-point in Wilde studies in the second half of the twentieth century. Finally, Merlin Holland's *The Wilde Album* and the NRF *Album Wilde* edited by Holland and Jean Gattégno offer a dazzling variety of Wildean images and a lucid and original commentary on the life and work which make them mandatory reading, too.

Introduction: The Iconic Oscar

O scar Wilde is a curiously suitable subject for a volume published by the National Portrait Gallery. Not only do portraits, those of Dorian Gray and of Willie Hughes, feature centrally – eponymously, indeed – in two of his most original works; representations of him, drawn, written, painted and photographed, occupy a highly significant place in his life. Wilde was not only one of the most illustrious, but also one of the most illustrated, of authors. This was no accident. He holds a singular place in the history of publicity, quite apart from his contributions to intellectual and artistic life. He was a pioneer of celebrity, fashioning and re-fashioning his image, until eventually, as with one of the most famous of his own creations, image and reality fatally parted company. His public career was brief – a bare twenty years, starting at Oxford, where he first began to have a public existence, and ending in a blaze of poisonous publicity with his incarceration in Pentonville, after which he was air-brushed out of the Victorian picture – but every phase of it is chronicled in a series of consecutive images which form an exemplary narrative, almost (*mutatis mutandis*) a secular Life of the Saints.

To say that before his fall Oscar Wilde knew and was known to everyone of importance in literary and social circles in both London and Paris is simply to state the truth; he had a wider fame in America

Oscar Wilde, Elliott & Fry, 1881

One feature, widely remarked upon, is fully apparent in all the photographs of Wilde: the eyes, what Pearson calls Wilde's 'magnificent eyes'. He goes on to point out that they 'constantly changed colour under their heavy lids: or so at least the biographer must write of them for people who knew him well have described them as blue, green-yellow, hazel, brown-and-gold ... the majority favouring blue flecked with gold.' Robbie Ross said they were light china blue, Alfred Douglas, green; the American socialite Anna de Brémont, covering all bets, describes them as 'pale blue, with golden flecks around the iris that changed strangely until the light within them seemed to turn to green'.

and Britain as a more or less buffoonish celebrity thanks to Gilbert's caricature of him as Bunthorne, the greenery-yallery, Grosvenor Gallery poet of *Patience*. However, to speak of Wilde's personal circle is more difficult. He set his cap at entering high society, and he achieved his object rapidly and relatively effortlessly. He remained in society, albeit often at an uneasy angle to it, until his downfall and trial, the most spectacular society scandal of the nineteenth – and perhaps any other – century. Thereafter he was an outcast and an exile, pointedly excluded from any contact with the men and women who had once so assiduously courted his company (should they chance to cross his path in the European watering holes where he was occasionally to be glimpsed). There were in fact two, not to say three, distinct circles in his adult, English, life, the social, the artistic and the sexual, and it is a curious and fascinating aspect of his life that he felt impelled to try to interpenetrate them, to make the public private and the private public, with catastrophic results. There were, in addition, a completely different, Anglo-Irish circle in his early years, and a somewhat shadowy European one after his trial. Most sombrely of all, he took up residence while in prison, as he remarks in *De Profundis*, in yet another circle: the Fifth Circle of Dante's Hell.

A brief sketch of his life will put some of this in context. He was born on 16 October 1854 in Dublin, the second child of Dr William Wilde, a distinguished ear surgeon and amateur archaeologist, and his wife Jane. They christened him Oscar Fingal O'Flahertie Wills Wilde. He was educated at Portora Royal School for Boys in Enniskillen, and then, from the age of seventeen, at Trinity College Dublin, where he fell under the influence of the egregious classics professor, socialite and virtuoso conversationalist, the Reverend John Pentland Mahaffy. In 1874 he won a demyship to Magdalen College, Oxford, where he studied, with great distinction, for four years. Then, in a surprising transformation, the dazzling scholar, winner of the most brilliant First in Classics of his year as well as the Newdigate Prize for Poetry, became a cameo star of the London social scene, notorious for his eccentric garments, his troubadorial devotion to certain cult beauties of the day and his languid promotion of the aesthetic movement. In the first of the many transformations that would characterise his life, the sturdy bowler-hatted, check-suited young Oxonian was replaced overnight, it would seem, by a long-haired, knee-breeched, velvet-jacketed dreamer, draped over a sofa, book in hand, eyes bent in ethereal contemplation.

In fact, he had been in training for the role: his triumph at the May Ball at Oxford when he appeared as Prince Rupert encouraged him to wear the same seventeenth-century outfit in the salons he so eagerly frequented on first arriving in London. It was then an obvious step to invent his own fancy dress. As for the aesthetic philosophy, this too was something which, while a perfectly sincerely held intellectual position, was developed into a consciously exaggerated and provocative stance at Oxford. He came to London trailing clouds of controversy.

His remark while a second-year student that he was finding it difficult to live up to his blue china achieved exactly what it had been meant to achieve: instant notoriety. Dean Burgon had denounced it from the pulpit of Oxford University Church: 'There has crept into the cloistered shades a form of heathenism which it is our bounden duty to fight against and to crush out if possible.' A little later, at the age of twenty-three, while still at Magdalen, he had made sufficient personal impact to be the model of the leading character in a novel, *The Mirage*, by Gordon Fleming, in which he appears as Claude Davenant: 'he spoke like a man who had studied expression. He listened like one accustomed to speak.'

It has been pointed out that, lacking money (his father had left very little), Wilde's only hope of self-advancement was by his wits. Luck, of course, played its part; sharing a house with the society portrait painter Frank Miles gave him contact with the Professional Beauties – supreme among them Lillie Langtry, whom he so publicly hymned in many a sonnet and triolet. They and serious actresses such as Ellen Terry and Sarah Bernhardt whom he equally lauded, were flattered and charmed by his attentions, extravagantly harmless as they were, and encouraged him. His foot was on the first rung of the ladder of celebrity.

It was evident from this early moment in his career that his desire for fame was an imperative to which he would submit without undue concern for his dignity. In fact, there was in his character a fundamental sense of self-worth, in addition to a basic good humour – those closely connected qualities – that somehow enabled him to transcend what in another man might have been preposterous. There was never any doubt that his current manifestation, whatever it might be, was – to use a word that reverberates powerfully and finally tragically through his career – a pose, nor that the poser was every bit as amused by it as the beholder.

If the purpose of the aesthetic pose had been to gain attention, it succeeded beyond all reasonable expectation. As early as 1880, when he had been in London for a bare year, Wilde was the identifiable model for two characters portrayed on the West End stage. The first was Scott Ramsey in *Where's the Cat?* by James Albery, played by a major luminary of the acting profession, Herbert Beerbohm Tree, later to be the owner of Her Majesty's Theatre; the second, in 1881, Lambert Streyke in *The Colonel* by Frank Burnand, the editor of *Punch*, in the pages of which he was also regularly satirised: 'And many a maiden will mutter,/ When Oscar looms large on her sight/ "He's quite consummately utter,/ As well as too utterly quite."' It was Gilbert and Sullivan's spoof *Patience* (1881), however, which took Wilde into the stratosphere of celebrity. The character of Reginald Bunthorne was instantly perceived as a satire on Wilde, to the degree that when the play's producer, Richard D'Oyly Carte, that master of razzmatazz, took the production to America, he invited Wilde to give a parallel lecture tour on matters aesthetical. Not in the least put out by being the butt of Gilbert's Philistine humour ('Caricature is the tribute which mediocrity pays to genius', he remarked, somewhat disingenuously, since he was actually making a caricature of himself), Wilde actively encouraged the comparison, appearing at a performance of the show identically attired to the actor playing Bunthorne; he was greeted with applause, a sound always pleasing to his ears.

OSCAR WILDE
Napoleon Sarony,
1882

Although Wilde would not be described, then or now, as handsome – the features are almost too full, even at this early age, before he had fleshed out, and the overall effect is boneless – there is no question that the camera loves him, and that the feeling is entirely mutual.

There was much more of it to follow, as he pursued a triumphant course around America, swiftly adapting his material to the appetite of his audience: his first lecture, 'The English Renaissance', over-long and over-theoretical, was replaced with 'Decorative Arts', then 'The House Beautiful', which made an unexpected hit with the miners of Colorado. There was a certain hysteria surrounding his appearances: in scenes that anticipate performances of *The Rocky Horror Show* a hundred years later, sixty Harvard undergraduates arrived in knee breeches when he spoke in Boston; at Yale there were two hundred thus attired. He retaliated by appearing in evening dress. The rest of the audience were far from pleased by this, so he became ever more sartorially extravagant. His message was taken seriously: America, even more than Britain, was ready for the anti-Victorian revolution in design that, inspired by Morris and Ruskin, Wilde was helping to usher in, promoting light and air over the dark heaviness of the mid-century, away from the Gothic, towards the Mediterranean.

Financially he was hugely rewarded for his efforts, surrounded by secretaries and servants and fêted wherever he went; the tally in column inches was considerable, the tone of the comment for the most part one of affectionate mockery. In Montreal he saw his name on a billboard six foot high. In another strikingly modern manifestation, he attached his name to various products, endorsing among other products, Madame Fontaine's Bosom Beautifier. He was also photographed in New York by the crown prince of portrait photographers, Napoleon Sarony, who took at least twenty-seven separate poses of him. It was a real photo shoot, à la *Vogue*, with a whole wardrobe department in attendance. Wilde appears in a fur-lined coat in which he looks like an adventurer, exotic, very masculine; in breeches and stockings with patent pumps, a little archaic. This was his English Renaissance mode. There is a sequence in velvet jacket and waistcoat, others in dinner jacket and breeches and in smoking jacket with quilted lapels, brocaded, with toggled buttons (see page 11). His long hair is parted in the middle, a feature of which his mother disapproved. A final sequence has him in operatic broad-brimmed hat and cloak. He wears an excessively large ring on the little finger of his left hand. The most famous head shot is slightly soft in focus, dreamy, romantic. Generally, the sitter looks at the viewer with a direct, frank and somewhat intimate gaze.

Whether these – or any other – photographs convey the real physical impact of the man is in doubt. The reason is provided by Edward Marjoribanks (by no stretch of the imagination a friendly witness) in his *Life of Lord Carson*: 'None of the photographs reveal even a hint of the strange charm which he is able to exercise … the smile changes everything.' Nowhere in these photographs does Wilde so much as hint at a smile; no doubt he was self-conscious about revealing his discoloured teeth.

Mutability is the key. Perhaps the most curious feature of the many manifestations of Wilde is the sheer unlikeliness of the raw material. Toweringly tall, striking, not to say unmistakable, plump, with long thin legs, he is very hard to disguise. The *New York Tribune* noted the disparity between the reality of Oscar Wilde and what he was peddling: 'his eyes are bright and quick – not at all like those of one given to perpetual musing on the ineffably beautiful and true. Instead of having a small delicate hand only fit to caress a lily, his fingers are long and when doubled up would form a fist that would hit a hard knock, should an occasion arise for the owner to descend to that kind of argument …' Yet he allows himself to be – in a phrase that he would not recognise – 'made over' in a way that would draw the admiration of a Madonna or a Cher or any of our contemporary, constantly mutating icons.

The next look was soon to follow. When Wilde returned from America, he went straight to Paris to write *The Duchess of Padua*, the play commissioned from him by the American actress Mary Anderson, and of course, he needed a new image. He found what he was looking for in the Louvre: a bust of Nero, his hair arranged in short bouffant curls; this coiffure he immediately adopted. Gone were the knee breeches, gone the velvet jacket. Instead he wore an elegant white suit. The impression is of a somewhat camp, well-heeled *flâneur*. Wilde had intended to conquer French literary society, nestling at the feet of his heroes (as he had in America, laying a chaste hand on Walt Whitman's knee), but the littérateurs were not so easily won over. That steat gossip Edmond Goncourt had no time for him at all: 'cet individu au sexe douteux, au langage de cabotin, au récits blagueurs' (this person of doubtful sex, hammy language and pretentious statements). Victor Hugo fell asleep during their conversation, pardonably, perhaps, since he was eighty-one. Verlaine, to Wilde shockingly ugly and dirty, was annoyed that his absinthe glass was not continually replenished. Wilde did not waste his time, however: he confirmed his friendship with Sarah Bernhardt, and he wrote the play. Alas, Mary Anderson rejected it, and he was suddenly penniless. He immediately undertook a British lecture tour, much less profitable than the American one. Meanwhile, his early play, *Vera*, opened and closed in rapid succession, to the delight of the same press whose favourite he had so recently been.

It was while he was in Dublin in 1883, lecturing on 'The House Beautiful', that Wilde met and impressed the twenty-year-old Constance Mary Lloyd, a demure, violet-eyed beauty who was staying with her Irish relatives. Their courtship proceeded at some distance, but their mutual attraction grew strongly, and soon their wedding took place, a relatively low-key affair, given the groom's propensity for publicity (the *Irish Times* commented that Wilde 'looked less like George IV than usual ... the modern blue morning frock and grey trousers rather took away from the character'). The bride was exquisitely attired; she appeared radiant, crowned with myrtle. The marriage was a great success to begin with; the romance and the sexual ardour were real as long as they lasted. The Wildes soon moved into the house in Tite Street, Chelsea, which was held to be the epitome of the House Beautiful on which Wilde had so eloquently lectured. Designed by Godwin, it exemplified all the light, airy qualities espoused by the English Renaissance Movement. In quick succession, Constance bore two sons, Cyril and Vyvyan. Wilde was now perceived as a proud paterfamilias. He was, as Merlin Holland sharply puts it, 'hovering dangerously on the edge of respectability'. In 1887 he became the editor of a new magazine, the *Woman's World*, which gave him a steady income and a formal position

OSCAR WILDE, Sydney Prior Hall, 1889

In the public imagination, Wilde had passed from being a silly great big boy in breeches, to being the sinister importer of filthy French ideas. In cartoons from the period, he is generally represented as an extravagant, portly, not to say porky, figure, encircled in the smoke emanating from his cigarette, no doubt murmuring sinful suggestions.

within the literary world. 'It re-established him', in Holland's words, 'as a front-line writer; it relieved the acute financial pressures; and above all it gave him some of those "finest, rarest moments" for "literature", effectively kick-starting him into the great creative years of his life.'

Wilde's own work began to be published in that same year (his *Poems* had been privately printed in 1880, and though admired in some quarters had had an unhappy history; his presentation copy of it was rejected by an overwhelming vote of the Oxford Union, and when Frank Miles's clergyman father read it Wilde was expelled from the house they shared). *The Canterville Ghost* was his first book to appear, in 1887, followed by *Lord Arthur Saville's Crime* the same year; *The Happy Prince and Other Tales* appeared in 1888. All, especially the last-named, were warmly received. The first of Wilde's intellectual provocations of the late Victorian establishment was *The Decay of Lying*, published in 1889, the year in which he retired from the editorship of the *Woman's World*.

Lying may have been uppermost in Wilde's mind because he had from 1887 been living the double life which would eventually destroy him, but which was also the source of so much that was original in his work. It seems that the arrival of the seventeen-year-old Robert Ross as a paying guest at Tite Street that year awoke in Wilde those proclivities which had so far been dormant; his sexual feelings for his wife had not, it appears, survived her two pregnancies. From that time forward he conducted a series of clandestine relationships with young men – Ross himself and then later the young poet John Gray – as he drifted further and further away from the domestic ambit. Meanwhile, his work was developing from the merely provocative to the downright notorious: *The Picture of Dorian Gray*, appearing first in *Lippincott's Magazine* (1890), then, slightly toned down, in hard covers, created a violent controversy between those (like Conan Doyle) who viewed it as a moral tract in which wickedness is finally punished, and those who regarded it as corrupting in itself, with its decadent themes so alien to the wholesome ideals of Victorian society.

As if to confirm the xenophobes' worst suspicions, Wilde now took off again for the *fons et origo* of all corruption, Paris, to write a play for

OSCAR WILDE AND LORD ALFRED 'BOSIE' DOUGLAS
Gillman & Co., probably May 1893

Wilde and Bosie's relationship was to some extent monstrous, and certainly contributed largely to Wilde's downfall and premature death. However, it was without question a *folie à deux*, an entirely mutual affair; the essential difference being the obvious one, that Wilde was a genius and a great spirit and Bosie was neither.

Sarah Bernhardt. He was greeted with much more respect and enthusiasm by the French literary set, by whom he was this time round lionised. Here he wrote *Salomé*, a piece of scented and bedizened symbolist drama, which despite sometimes seeming to betray excessive recourse to the thesaurus, exercises a curious power in performance. Wholesome, it is not, however, and it is scarcely surprising that the Lord Chamberlain found an excuse for aborting its London production, invoking an ancient law forbidding representation of biblical characters on the stage.

The momentum of Wilde's life was now quickening. Artistically and financially, he was about to enter his golden period. In 1890 the distinguished actor-manager George Alexander took what might seem to be the obvious step of commissioning the greatest conversationalist of his age to write a modern play. The following year Wilde wrote what was to become *Lady Windermere's Fan*. Privately, he had met the young man who proved to be his nemesis, Lord Alfred Douglas, twenty-one at the time of their meeting and the youngest son of John Sholto Douglas, the 8th Marquess of Queensberry. Their acquaintance grew until, in 1892, Douglas (known as Bosie to his family and friends) asked the older man for help over an attempt to blackmail him. He had been a highly and indiscreetly active homosexual for some years; this was not the first time he had been trapped. It seems that it was then that he and Wilde became lovers. The relationship was one of mutual infatuation, but sex was not at the heart of it, and Bosie soon introduced Wilde to the underworld of male prostitutes with which he had long been familiar. This world enthralled Wilde, as much for its danger and otherness as for any inherent sexual satisfaction. It thrilled him to emerge, blinking, from those environs, and enter a fashionable drawing room, or the foyer of a theatre where one of his plays was running. Even more thrilling was to bring an inhabitant of that underworld with him into the glittering purlieus of the great and the good, to the Café Royal or to Kettner's restaurant. These transgressions of the sacred barriers of class were widely noted, though no public comment was made at the time.

Although Wilde scrupulously maintained his relationship with his children – sometimes coming to them in their nursery direct from one of his low-life encounters – he was now essentially a visitor in his own home. Constance was dutifully at his side at first nights and on social occasions, looking appropriately radiant, and they were duly reported in the gossip columns as a golden couple in the nineteenth century's equivalent of *Hello!* and *OK!* magazines; most often, however, he would deliver her back to Tite Street and continue on to one or other of his haunts. With Bosie he travelled the world as a sexual tourist. Their personal association had become increasingly stormy – unilaterally so, since it was Bosie's hysterical petulance when denied anything which defined its tone, with Wilde in the role of placator. He struggled to maintain his literary output, now more necessary than ever, since he was invariably the one who picked up the tab; extraordinarily, in view of Bosie's incessant demands on him, Wilde managed to produce four more plays and a number of poems in prose during this period. Their friendship was highly visible and the cause of much comment, not least from Bosie's father, who, as part of the running battle he had maintained with his children from their earliest years, determined to smash both Bosie and Wilde. His attentions grew more and more threatening, culminating in his delivery of what has been graphically described as a phallic bouquet of market vegetables to the stage door of the St James's Theatre on the triumphant First Night of *The Importance of Being Earnest* in 1895, following this up with an open card left at the club of which both he and Wilde were members, the Albemarle, stating: 'To Oscar Wilde, posing somdomite [sic]'. Beleaguered, exhausted and angry, Wilde took the suicidal option of suing Queensberry for criminal libel, a course passionately urged on him by Bosie, who saw this as the ideal method for finally smashing his father. Denying any truth in Queensberry's allegation (anyway a somewhat indefensible proposition; where is the libel in being accused of posing as something?), instead of pressing the advantage against the accused, Wilde found himself in the dock defending both his work and his conduct under the unrelenting cross-examination of Queensberry's counsel, Edward Carson.

When it became apparent that the defence had marshalled a great deal of potentially incriminating evidence from boy prostitutes, Wilde privately informed his counsel, Sir Edward Clarke, of an incident in which he had been turned out of a hotel in the middle of the night with a young man. Clarke urged immediate withdrawal of the case. The Crown Prosecutors issued a warrant for Wilde's arrest, apparently delaying its issue to give Wilde the opportunity to flee the country. He, however, chose to stay, and was duly apprehended at the Cadogan Hotel in Sloane Street. When his case came to court, he was tried alongside Alfred Taylor, the 'madam' of a male brothel that Wilde had frequented. The first trial produced a hung verdict, and a re-trial was ordered. Wilde was given bail and was again urged by friends to escape; again he refused. The strange impression of paralysis, almost of sleep-walking suggested by Wilde's behaviour expresses the feeling he later described of playing out a role in some preordained tragedy; in one of many odd uncanny premonitions Wilde had during his life, he had told his friends twenty years earlier at Trinity 'that there is nothing he would rather do than go down to posterity as the defendant in such a case as *Regina* v *Wilde*.' A regular frequenter of clairvoyants, he had, after the First Night of *A Woman of No Importance*, in 1893, tendered his hand anonymously to the famous palmist Cheiro who told him: 'the left hand is the hand of a king, but the right is that of a king who will send himself into exile.' Questioning the inevitability of this destiny, Wilde did not wait for a reply but gave the answer himself: 'Fate does not keep road-menders on her highway.'

The third trial, despite a balanced and reasonable summing-up by the judge, drawing attention to the unsafeness of some of the evidence (which encouraged the Solicitor-General, prosecuting, to murmur to Edward Clarke, defending, 'you'll dine your man in Paris tonight') resulted in a unanimous verdict of guilty. The judge, with savage relish, imposed the severest sentence available to him, two years hard labour, 'in my view … totally inadequate for a case such as this'. The cries of 'Shame!' heard in the court, protesting at the severity of the sentence, contrasted with the scenes of rejoicing in the street, where, it is said, prostitutes danced; the rent boys were killing their business.

Wilde was sent first to Pentonville Prison, then to Wandsworth, and finally Reading Gaol, where the brutal Colonel J. Isaacson was in time replaced by the relatively enlightened Major Nelson. The privations he endured during his two years' imprisonment were extreme. For much of the time he was ill. He focused his energies, such as they were, on composing the immensely long letter to Alfred Douglas, known in its published form as *De Profundis*, reviewing the events that had led to his present predicament. Three times he appeared in public: twice at bankruptcy proceedings, where his physical condition – emaciated, short-haired and lightly bearded – was reported by the press, once when he was transferred by rail from Wandsworth to Reading. Changing trains at Clapham Junction he was recognised by passengers, who formed a jeering crowd. One man spat at him. Fortunately this scene, which haunted Wilde for the rest of his short life, was not reported.

Wilde remained eminently newsworthy. The trial and his early days in prison were illustrated for the readers of popular newspapers by a series of line drawings and linocuts which form a stark contrast to the opulent images of his former life. In court, he is represented as lolling somewhat insolently in the dock; in the – imaginary – scenes in prison, he is shown having his hair shorn: 'The locks that have been admired and admired by society, alas! How they have fallen.' Bosie claimed, in a letter to the Secretary of State, that fifty pressmen had been allowed to witness Wilde exercising in the prison yard, but there is no corroborative evidence for this. Newspapers continued to report on his progress inside, in largely sympathetic tones, and his release from prison was soberly chronicled in *The Morning*, which stated that he looked very well: 'His build and general appearance were – as of old – distinguished and attractive. In short, Oscar Wilde of today is the Oscar Wilde, so far as appearance goes.' The notion of there being such an entity as *the* Oscar Wilde may have afforded him some wry amusement.

On his release, at the age of forty-two, Wilde swiftly left the country and never returned. The remaining three years of his life were spent in a kind of limbo, socially, artistically and emotionally, as he drifted across Europe, finally, somehow inevitably, ending up in Paris. At first, he hoped to lead a hermitic existence in an isolated part of Brittany, but his old appreciation of the pleasures of wine, food and company, particularly that of attractive young men, asserted itself. The inner core of his band of friends was loyal to him, valiantly trying to ensure that his body and soul remained together, and encouraging him to write again. In fact, he only published one work after his release, *The Ballad of Reading Gaol* (1898), which he completed almost immediately (the idea for it, he said, had come to him as he sat in the dock at his trial). His genius for story-telling never left him, but he chose to exercise it in conversational form; on several occasions he sold the plot for the same play to different people. He kept up a vigorous correspondence with many friends, and these letters – perfectly composed, funny, profound and revealing – constitute a major aspect of his literary legacy, and partly explain why Wilde's personality is almost as vivid to posterity as it was to his contemporaries.

Wilde's mother had died while he was in prison; his wife, Constance, who had changed her name to the family name of Holland to protect herself and the children, provided him with a small allowance, conditional on his refusing ever to see Lord Alfred Douglas again. This condition Wilde refused to accept, and he was briefly reunited with that impossible young man when they shared a villa near Naples. Finally, in an exquisitely ironic touch, Bosie left him, when Lady Queensberry promised to give both Bosie and Wilde an allowance on condition that he never saw Wilde again, a condition which he honoured. Nor did Wilde ever again see Constance, who predeceased him; nor, to his infinite grief, was he ever allowed to see the children, or to communicate with them in any way.

OSCAR WILDE, unknown photographer, spring 1900
On the steps of St Peter's, Rome

Wilde was often photographed in front of monuments, looking portly and melancholy, 'like an unfrocked Lateran Bishop', as he said of himself, though perhaps the phrase 'exiled monarch' better describes the impression; these photographs of a dispossessed Titan have a peculiar poetry about them.

As he wandered through his last years, shunned by the respectable middle classes *en vacances,* shamelessly approaching former acquaintances for money, Wilde took photographs and was himself photographed. Wilde's sense of the absurd, so central to his work, became the keynote of his life, and accompanied him right up to the death which he had so long anticipated. 'I am dying beyond my means', he said. 'I will never outlive the century. The English would never stand it.' He died on 30 November 1900, at the age of forty-six. Once Wilde had been cleaned up, Maurice Gilbert, one of the more lasting of his swains from the previous couple of years, took a photograph of him, looking thin and noble, like a knight on a coffin, the final haunting image in a life of images.

Carefully supervised by Robbie Ross, his executor, Wilde's rehabilitation commenced almost immediately, despite the awful shadow that his trial and imprisonment cast over the whole post-Victorian scene. *De Profundis* appeared in 1905. *Salomé* had been performed, triumphantly, by Lugné-Poë in Paris in 1896, and almost immediately set to music – very nearly word for word – by Richard Strauss, creating a resounding scandal that Wilde would have enormously enjoyed. The other plays were soon revived in Britain, particularly *The Importance of Being Earnest. An Ideal Husband*, *A Woman of No Importance* and *Lady Windermere's Fan* were intermittently revived, generally as examples of high camp, gorgeously apparelled by Cecil Beaton and other equally flamboyant designers. Later, from the 1970s, they were rediscovered, in productions by Phillip Prowse and Peter Hall, as the complex and provocative pieces that they are. Wilde's stock has risen and risen, in a paradoxical (and perfectly Wildean) development both emblematically, as a gay martyr, and practically, as his profound wit, his dramatic genius and his irresistible story-telling came to be seen for their own merits, away from the shadow of his tragic destiny. His work, of course, is his supreme monument, while his fate has made his life one of the best-known stories of the modern age. He has been memorialised in two radically different sculptures: the massive and epic tomb that Jacob Epstein conceived for the transfer of his remains to Père Lachaise cemetery in Paris in 1909, and Maggi Hambling's *jeu d'esprit* just off the Strand, in which a smoking, green Oscar emerges from the slab of his coffin, clearly in mid-jest. Epstein's conception is altogether more heroic, not to say monolithic: Wilde appears as a 'flying demon angel' on the side of a great rectangular catafalque, his features somehow Asiatic, maybe Egyptian. Unlikely as this may appear as a representation of the languid, perennially droll author, it served for many years as a rallying point for homosexual men; touching messages were scrawled on it, 'Jean aime Pierre' or 'Patrice, Louis à toujours'.

Epstein had endowed his demon-angel with a spectacularly pendulous set of testicles, which were initially covered up, at the insistence of the cemetery authorities, with a bronze fig leaf. This was wrested off and stolen by Aleister Crowley in 1914, exposing the full genital splendour, which was finally demolished by two English ladies who smashed the testicles off in 1961. Such posthumous comedy is exquisitely apt to the man who brought a witty smile to the lips even of those most determined to resist him. Somewhat before the Hambling statue, paid for by public subscription, was installed, there came an act of retributive justice that Wilde himself could scarcely have imagined as he died, neglected, impoverished, despised. In the year of the centenary of his trial, 1995, a plaque to him was unveiled in Poets' Corner in Westminster Abbey. That his fame should finally have come to rest in the national home of dead heroes, and then – how this would have satisfied him! – under the noble name of Poet, might have brought a tear to his eye, as it did to many for whom a great wrong was finally, if not righted, at least atoned for.

BEFORE
LONDON

SIR WILLIAM (1815–76)
AND LADY WILDE (1821–96)

Wilde's parents cut striking and distinguished figures in Dublin society, though they were not quite at the centre of it, their eccentricity and originality setting them somewhat apart. Wilde's father, William, was a man of extraordinary intellectual range, a doctor who had specialised in ophthalmic and aural surgery, travelled widely and written books on subjects medical, topographical, historical and archaeological. He was the medical advisor and assistant commissioner to the great Irish Census of 1851, collating statistics for ear and eye disease; in 1863 he was appointed Surgeon Oculist in Ireland to Queen Victoria. A year later, he was knighted; a year earlier, he had received the Order of the Polar Star from the Governor of Uppsala in Sweden. In 1851 he had married Jane Elgee (born in 1821, a statistic she preferred to forget), when she was thirty and he was six years older. She was famous in her own right

SIR WILLIAM WILDE, after J.H. Maguire, 1847

It is interesting to note the evolution in William's demeanour from the plump, soft-eyed, soft-mouthed twenty-eight-year-old of drawings and photographs, in whom his son Oscar's features can so readily be discerned, to the figure of his later years, seeming to bear no resemblance whatever to him.

for her nationalistic writings which, under the *nom de guerre* of Speranza, appeared in *The Nation*, the organ of the Young Ireland movement. Her rally to arms written at the height of the famine, 'Jacta Alea Est', had been instrumental in the suppression of the magazine; after that she concentrated on translating grand romantic novels from German and French: Lamartine's *The Wanderer and His Home*; Meinhold's *Sidonia The Sorceress*.

The year of their nuptials, Wilde published *Irish Popular Superstitions*; he and Speranza were united in their commitment to Ireland, its history and identity.

Physically, the relationship was an arresting one to behold: Speranza a Junoesque six-foot tall; her husband rather shorter and distinctly simian in appearance. He could almost be a cousin of the Marquess of Queensberry. 'Pithecoid' is the adjective devised by Hesketh Pearson to describe his appearance: and there is something of Mr Hyde about him, a horrible, brutish raw energy in the face, a feral quality which must have been confirmed for his contemporaries by the strong smell of unwashed skin reputed – however unjustly – to emanate from him. The eyes are sunken, the chin weak, the hair proliferates around and

JANE FRANCESCA WILDE
'As Speranza of *The Nation*'
After Stephen Catterson Smith, *c*.1848

William's marriage to Jane was a great love match, despite his extremes of mood. 'I love and suffer', she wrote, with characteristic expansiveness, 'this is all I am conscious of now and thus my great soul is prisoned within a woman's destiny – nothing interests me beyond the desire to make *him* happy.'

particularly beneath his chin; he appears to have gone native while remaining happily ensconced in Merrion Square. In fact, in person, he was a fine conversationalist and had considerable charm, not least in the sexual sphere. Before he married he had fathered three children, whom he openly acknowledged and of whom he was immensely fond, and supported financially; the fondness was warmly reciprocated. Speranza bore him three children – William, Oscar and Isola – all of whom benefited from the liberal attitudes to children within the household: when visitors came to their mother's gatherings (*conversazione*, she called them), they were allowed to attend. Her second son bore the strongest evidence of his mother's nationalism in his name: Oscar Fingal (after the names of the son and father of the legendary Gaelic warrior and bard Oisín) and O'Flahertie after his father's ancestors. 'Is that not grand and Ossianic?' she asked. He was not an unusual boy in any way, and pursued an amiable, dreamy life, both in town and in their country retreat; nor was he his mother's favourite. Willie, extrovert and quick, was her darling; Oscar, she said, was only good at growing fat. In time, the balance of affection would change.

The most dramatic event of Oscar's childhood, when he was ten years old, was the libel trial brought by a certain Mary Travers against Speranza. Wilde's father had treated the nineteen-year-old for an ear infection, had become friendly with her and finally had seduced her. Two years after the event, after she had extracted the money for a passage to Australia from him, she accused him in means of anonymous pamphlets addressed to Dr and Mrs Quilp and signed 'Speranza', of her 'ruin', asserting that he had raped her while she was under the influence of chloroform. Jane Wilde first seized the pamphlets, then wrote to Mary's father alerting him to his daughter's behaviour ('you may not be aware of [her] disreputable conduct at Bray'). Mary found the letter, and sued Lady Wilde (as she now was). During the trial, Lady Wilde behaved with magnificent disdain for the whole business (though nobody doubted for a moment that Wilde had seduced his former patient), but the verdict went against them; Sir William was saddled with costs of £2,000. The whole event sounds a curious pre-echo to

Oscar's trial, some thirty years later; libel was the issue which scuppered both generations of Wildes. In fact, Sir William seemed little distressed by the case, continuing to publish (as did Speranza), but he was profoundly affected by the death of all his daughters, first Isola, in 1867, at the age of nine, of a fever, and then, in 1871, both his illegitimate daughters, Mary and Emily, at the same time: seeing that her dress had caught fire, one daughter rushed to the aid of the other, and both were caught up in the flames. He now rarely appeared in public, and finally he took to his bed and died at the age of sixty-one.

Speranza behaved during her husband's last days with characteristic indifference to convention; Oscar reported that a black-veiled woman appeared at the house every day and was allowed to go and sit silently by Sir William's bedside. 'Not one woman in a thousand would have tolerated her presence, but my mother allowed it, because she knew my father loved this woman and felt that it must be a joy and a comfort to have her there beside his dying bed.' Oscar himself was by now a student at Oxford; his father, to Oscar's infinite regret, did not live to witness his academic triumphs.

The curious mess of Sir William's will meant that, before long, Lady Wilde transferred her establishment to London. A friend reported visiting her at the time of the move, as servants wept and bailiffs moved in, finding her lying on a sofa in the drawing room, reading Aeschylus's *Prometheus Bound*: 'She would not let me slip in a word of condolence, but seemed very anxious that I should share her entire admiration for the beauties of the Greek tragedian which she was reading', a scene which perfectly reflects her son's priorities, and oddly evokes the scene of Wilde's arrest at the Cadogan Hotel some eighteen years later.

For a while, after he had been jettisoned from Frank Miles's house in Tite Street, Wilde lived with his mother. When he married, Constance took warmly to her mother-in-law, and this devotion never waned, even through the trial and the subsequent imprisonment. When Wilde was given bail after the second trial and was denied admission to every hotel in London, he finally turned to his mother. She, in a sadly misjudged intervention, sided with Alfred Douglas in insisting that he should not quit the country. Speranza never believed the truth of the charges against Wilde, seeing the trial as simply another treacherous manifestation of Albion's Imperial Might. While he was in prison she hoped for a letter from him, but it never came: he was allowed one only every three months. For her part, she refrained from writing to him because she dreaded her letters being returned. At the beginning of 1896 she became ill with bronchitis and wrote to the authorities to ask if he might be released to visit her for one last time; the wish was refused. She died in February 1896. Constance Wilde (now Holland) returned from Genoa to break the news gently to Wilde. In *De Profundis* Wilde says that 'her death was so terrible to me that I, once a lord of language, have no words in which to express my anguish and my shame.' He felt that he had dragged the great name his parents had bequeathed him through the mud (forgetting that his father had once done pretty well in the same line).

Speranza was buried in Kensal Green Cemetery with no headstone, so, after seven years, the body was removed to an unknown grave.

SIR JOHN PENTLAND MAHAFFY (1839–1919)

_leaving Portora Royal School, Wilde went straight to Trinity College
Dublin, at the early but not unduly precocious age of seventeen.
His proven academic excellence was only enhanced by his studies
there; but its importance in his life is in its provision of a larger stage for
him to play on. The process of self-creation had begun at school; now
he absorbed various new essential elements. A powerful source of
these was in the flamboyant person of his tutor, the distinguished class-
icist, the Reverend John Pentland Mahaffy, at thirty-two a formidable
figure on the campus, and anywhere else. Known as The General, his
accomplishments straddled many spheres: Captain of the Trinity eleven
and a famous shot, he was also fluent in Hebrew as well as several
other languages. His knowledge of wines and cigars was fabled; the
toast of Anglo-Irish society, Mahaffy was assiduous in his cultivation of
the international great and the good, in which he was egregiously
successful, since his acquaintance included several reigning monarchs.

The young Wilde was naturally excited by the sheer projected
vividness of Mahaffy's personality, by the cut and thrust of his intellectual discourse and by his supreme social self-assurance. In time Wilde
would surpass him in all of these areas, with infinitely greater grace,
but Mahaffy was an ideal prototype for a young man intent on making
an impact.

Interestingly, Mahaffy had little or no interest in Ancient Rome,
with whose highly masculine, determinist world-view he might have
been expected to sympathise, preferring instead the much more
sophisticated philosophies of the Greeks, whose superiority he vigorously proclaimed: he seems in fact to have promoted a sort of muscu-
lar Hellenism. For Wilde it opened up a whole world of intellectual
experience and a conception of existence with which he found himself
profoundly in sympathy. His work and life were fundamentally

influenced by what he learned under Mahaffy, stylistically, politically, philosophically and, ultimately, sexually, though this last influence is more oblique. Mahaffy himself was the vigorously heterosexual father of two sons, but he had the courage – in the first edition of his book *Social Life in Greece from Homer to Menander*, a book whose proofs the young Wilde helped to correct – at least to allude to Greek homosexuality; by the second edition, the allusions were out. But when later, in his third year at Oxford, Wilde joined Mahaffy on a trip to Greece (his first) Mahaffy told him that 'I am going to make an honest pagan of you.' Paganism, he had said, resoundingly, was preferable to Popery, and it is this antithesis, of ancient Greece and papal Rome, which defined the struggle for the soul of the twenty-three-year-old Wilde. All his life he was drawn to the sensual and emotional aspect of Catholicism, its rituals and rubric. As so often in a life so continuously charged with significance, on his way home from Greece Wilde made a symbolic diversion to the Holy City at the behest of newly converted fellow-students, even meeting the Pope himself (Pius IX), who urged him to join his friends in the fold; but he held back from actual conversion, preferring, as always, both/and to either/or. (On his return, late, to Oxford, he was punished by the academic authorities: 'I was sent down – for being the first undergraduate to visit Olympus.') Mahaffy was able to boast that he had been able 'to cheat the devil of his due'.

Thereafter their paths diverged. Wilde came to see his former mentor whose High Tory anti-Nationalist stance had become grotesque, as politically ridiculous and over-strenuous socially. When he was editing the *Woman's World*, he reviewed Mahaffy's book about the art of conversation patronisingly, and the next book, *The Greek Life*, dismissively. Mahaffy for his part expressed nothing but contempt for Wilde after his demise: 'he was the one blot on my tutorship.' Wilde would be a very different Wilde however, without what he learned from Mahaffy.

Sir John Pentland Mahaffy, Fradelle & Young, *c*.1887

Mahaffy's conversation according to Wilde was that of 'a really great talker in a certain way ... an artist in vivid words and eloquent pauses', which is another way of saying that he was evidently quite a conversational bully. A typical sally is his remark to Wilde after he had secured his demyship to Magdalen: 'You're not quite clever enough for us here, Oscar. Better run up to Oxford.'

WALTER PATER (1839–94)
AND JOHN RUSKIN (1819–1900)

For Wilde, Oxford was a larger stage again, and an infinitely stimulating intellectual climate, where the idiosyncratic Hellenist Mahaffy was replaced by towering figures of the contemporary scene. The crucial influences were Walter Pater and John Ruskin, for Wilde opposed yet complementary prophets, as Richard Ellmann has vividly delineated them, both espousing the ideal of beauty, yet from entirely different points of view: Ruskin the apostle of its spiritual aspect, Pater the celebrator of sensation. The two men had radically different profiles within the university. Ruskin the Slade Professor of Art, at fifty-five by far the senior, was already an almost legendary figure, author of innumerable books, including *The Stones of Venice, Modern Painters* and *Unto This Last* (1860), whereas Pater, thirty-five years old, Fellow of Brasenose, was the author of only one book to date, the recent, highly controversial *Studies in the History of the Renaissance* (1873), whose ecstatic conclusion – 'A counted number of pulses is given to us only of a variegated dramatic life. How may we see in them all that is to be seen in them by the finest dramatic pulses? How can we pass most swiftly from point to point, and be present always at the focus where the greatest number of vital forces unite in their purest energy? To burn always with that hard gem-like flame, to maintain this ecstasy, is success in life' – had become the rallying call of a younger generation determined to cast off the straitjacket of mid-Victorian morality.

Wilde was drawn not only to the philosophies of both these men, but also to their prose styles: Ruskin's subtle, limpid, clear, Pater's suggestive, modulated, erotic. Pater's book, Wilde said, was 'my golden book … which has had such a strange influence on my life.' Wilde met Pater for the first time after sending him his review of the opening of the Grosvenor Gallery (his first published prose) and various poems; while still at Oxford he had sent examples of his work to various distinguished public men, including Gladstone, which was casting his net wide indeed. Pater was delighted with the review, sensing the arrival of an unqualified disciple. They met at Oxford, and began a friendship which was viewed with alarm by Wilde's contemporaries: Pater had been implicated in a university scandal in which he had ended a letter to an undergraduate with the phrase *'yours lovingly'*. This association only added to the general air of sexual ambiguity which surrounded the young Wilde.

In fact, Pater's influence on him was more stylistic than moral (the later Wilde would of course have vehemently rejected any such distinction), 'Why do you always write poetry?' Pater asked him. 'Why do you not write prose? Prose is so much more difficult.' Thenceforward Wilde cultivated the perfumed cadences of his master. Later he was to find Pater's own prose somewhat too studied, but its influence is everywhere to be found in Wilde's work. During the period of their intimacy, Pater had given him a copy of Théophile Gautier's *Mademoiselle de Maupin*, another work whose exquisite sensibility Wilde claimed as crucially formative. Despite their affable social acquaintance, Wilde was unimpressed by Pater's personal manner; Hesketh Pearson describes him as 'one of those timid, old-maidish scholarly recluses who, fearing even the uncertainties of marriage, preach the gospel of living dangerously. In Germany he would have sung the glories of the sword and superman. In England he hinted at forbidden fruit.' The implied comparison with Nietzsche is illuminating.

Although their paths scarcely crossed after Oxford, Wilde was enchanted to receive Pater's praise for his fairy story, *The Selfish Giant*: 'perfect in its kind … the whole, too brief, book [*The Happy Prince and Other Tales*] abounds with delicate touches and pure English.' By the time he was told of Pater's death, however, a certain disenchantment had set in: 'was he ever alive?' Wilde asked.

Wilde's feelings about Ruskin were quite different, illuminatingly so. While freely acknowledging Pater's influence, he was sparing of his

WALTER PATER
Elliott & Fry, 1890s

As a young man, Pater's
ugliness was so remarkable
that his fellow students
formed a Committee to
Consider What Could be
Done for the Improvement
of Pater's Personal Appearance. They finally settled
on a moustache, which he
duly grew.

admiration for him as an individual. Ruskin, on the other hand, excited
his esteem to a degree verging on hero worship. From 1874 he had
attended Ruskin's famous series of lectures on Florentine art, admiring
the searing eloquence of both matter and manner (by comparison,
Pater's murmured lectures were elusive in their impact: 'did you hear
my lecture?' asked Pater, after one. 'We overheard it', replied Wilde).
The young Wilde's enthusiasm led him to answer Ruskin's challenge to
the undergraduates to stop wasting their time on the sports field and do
something useful, like building a road. Wilde was there with the best of
them, perhaps not as often as he later claimed in his American lectures,
but there nonetheless, his coat off, sleeves rolled up, spade in hand – a
curious premonitory vision of the punitive hard labour he was later to
perform as a convict. (Richard Ellmann marvellously remarks that
'Wilde's life is as full of tragic prolepses as an Ibsen play'.) Ruskin
befriended the young Irishman who revered him as 'prophet ... priest
and ... poet' as he told him in a letter. They saw each other socially,

publicly and at Wilde's house after his marriage; when Vyvyan was born Wilde asked Ruskin to be his godfather. He sweetly declined, on grounds of advanced age: he was sixty-six (as it happens he just out-lived Wilde, dying the same year, 1900).

Ruskin's idealism, his social vision and his conception of practical beauty were central to Wilde's work and thinking, both in his early lectures in America and Britain and in his journalism, but even more explicitly in the 1891 essay, 'The Soul of Man Under Socialism', which expounds what is essentially an anarchist philosophy, insisting on the dignity and self-determination of the individual. It is a strand of Wilde's work and thought which is tougher and more vigorous than its generally languid surface often suggests. Pater died before Wilde's downfall; by 1895, Ruskin inhabited a mental twilight. It is interesting to speculate on how these supremely different exemplars might have reacted to it.

JOHN RUSKIN
Charles Lutwidge Dodgson ('Lewis Carroll'), c.1875

Despite reservations about certain of Ruskin's positions, Wilde regarded him unequivocally as 'one of the greatest men England has ever produced'.

LONDON

LILLIE LANGTRY (1853–1929)

F rank Miles was a much prized and skilful society portrait painter; when Wilde moved in with him, he placed himself close to the centre of an artistic circle that was heavily concerned with fashion and image, the theatre and journalism. It was not quite literary, not exactly the *beau monde*. It was, in fact, very much the world frequented by the Prince of Wales (the future Edward VII): raffish, hedonistic, socially competitive, an almost Balzacian world (it is interesting to note that the ambitious Lucien de Rubempré was one of Wilde's favourite characters in all of literature). Quintessentially characteristic of this world was the phenomenon of the Professional Beauties, among the first modern celebrities, famous above all for being famous. Something more than demi-mondaines, something less than respectable, their supreme representative was Mrs Lillie Langtry, born and brought up in Jersey, who burst upon the London scene in May of 1876. The many photographs of her which survive show exactly why she caused such a sensation: a freshness of complexion, a charm of demeanour, the intimation of a free spirit. Wilde immediately became a fan, collecting photographs and a painting of her before they met; their first encounter was later the same year, and they took to each other at once. He and Miles saw immediate possibilities for her promotion 'by pencil and pen'. They would make her the 'Joconde and Laura of the century'. They seem to have become chums, three young people on the make; Ellmann unexpectedly suggests that she and Wilde might have had an affair. His pose towards her was that of a lovesick troubadour: 'I remember we used to meet/By an ivied seat/And you warbled each pretty word/With the air of a bird.' Lillie's actual sex life was becoming far more earthy and real than anything implied in Wilde's swoony early verse: she became the mistress of the Prince of Wales, and then was made pregnant by another man (certainly not her patient husband Edward, who seemed

EMILIE CHARLOTTE 'LILLIE' LANGTRY, Henry van der Weyde, c.April 1885

Wilde said of Lillie Langtry, 'I would rather have discovered Mrs Langtry than have discovered America.'

perfectly content for her merely to bear his name, if not his children). She withdrew to Jersey to have the child, who was brought up there, out of sight. Her very public friendship with Wilde and Frank Miles continued: Oscar took her to lectures at King's College, where they were cheered by the students on their – generally late – arrival; he continued to advise her on her clothes. All in all he was a perfect gay friend, except that, apparently, he wasn't. Indeed, he seemed to be devastated by their occasional tiffs. Arriving at the theatre to find her there during one of these estrangements, he had to be taken home, sobbing, by Frank Miles. When love's course ran true, he carried a lily with him. It was all very good copy.

The question of What To Do With Lillie obsessed the Tite Street fraternity. It was Wilde who came up with the obvious solution: she should become an actress. This she duly did, achieving a modest success; then, inevitably, she crossed the Atlantic to expand her fame, happily at exactly the same time Wilde was riding the crest of his own personal wave.

He greeted her at the docks in New York at 4.30a.m. with a bunch of lilies, in what can only be described as fancy dress ('He was dressed as probably no man in the world has ever dressed before', said the *New York Times*, faithfully covering his every move); he reviewed her performance in *An Unequal Match* in ecstatic terms. They were perfect accomplices in publicity.

Lillie was among the first to whom he announced his engagement to Constance. From then on, he had a new muse, and besides, Lillie was well enough established for their partnership in promotion to be redundant. She appeared at the First Night of *Lady Windermere's Fan*, as Wilde's guest, having turned down the role of Mrs Erlynne, on the grounds that nobody would believe that she had a grown daughter; she was thirty-nine at the time. Thereafter they seem not to have met. There are reports of her peddling malicious gossip about his homosexuality; perhaps she felt that it made a mockery of his earlier devotion to her. After his release from prison, she pretended to have sent money to him, but, Ellmann baldly tells us, 'she never did'.

JAMES MCNEILL WHISTLER (1834–1903)

James McNeill Whistler, some twenty years older than Wilde, a commanding but always controversial figure in the artistic and social scene of the 1870s, was another visitor to Frank Miles's studio/salon in Tite Street; he too was one of the admirers of Lillie Langtry. He was, in fact, a neighbour; he lived up the road in the new house he had bought with money made from his Venetian pictures. His spectacular libel case against Ruskin – the great man had described his paintings as being nothing more than 'a pot of paint flung in the face of the public' – had left him bankrupt (though he had won, he had to pay costs). He had been forced to sell his famous White House, also in Tite Street. Later, when Wilde bought himself a house in the same street, Whistler advised him on the décor. In 1879, when they first met, Wilde had already expressed his enthusiasm for the painter's work in a review for a Dublin paper: Whistler immediately took to his young fan, and a sparring partnership – initially a genial one – sprang up between them, in which Wilde was generally and happily the fall guy.

Their style was equally contrasting: Whistler's sharp wit always contained an element of vinegar in it, and was invariably turned against someone or something, less butterfly – his famous monogram – than bee. It lacked the fanciful dimension of Wilde's, its good-humoured absurdity. Whistler meant to hurt; Wilde to amuse (and sometimes to instruct). For a while, they were sufficiently associated in the public mind to be joint models for the guyed aesthetes in *Patience*; George Grossmith playing Bunthorne was unmistakably modelled on Whistler. On his lecture tour of the United States, Wilde reported that when he described one of Whistler's Nocturnes in blue and gold to the miners in Leadville, 'they leaped to their feet and in their grand simple way swore that such things should not be.' So far, so cordial.

J. Mac Neil Whistler

JAMES ABBOTT MCNEILL WHISTLER
Harry Furniss, c.1880–1910

Wilde and Whistler must have made a curious pair; Whistler, tiny and dapper, with the air, said the painter Charles Ricketts, of a Hungarian bandmaster, Wilde, a physical giant by comparison, increasingly luxuriant in appearance and manner.

The relationship throve as long as it was dominated by Whistler; as Wilde grew into an increasingly considerable figure in his own right, the banter turned rough. Above all, Whistler resented Wilde's incursion into his own fiefdom, the world of art, upon which Wilde was expatiating with growing confidence and authority; Whistler darkly suspected Wilde of stealing his own carefully honed phrases and cavalier theories. 'I wish I had said that'. 'You will, Oscar, you will'. It is true that some of Wilde's paradoxes take remarks of Whistler's as a starting point. Generally, however, Wilde refines them and gives them a more general application than Whistler's limited focus. The older man's waxing resentment of the younger found its expression in an address delivered at the Royal Academy, the celebrated Ten O'Clock Lecture, in which he denounced Wilde's amateur theorising. Wilde replied airily: 'Mr Whistler is one of the very greatest masters of painting, in my opinion. And I may add that in this opinion, Mr Whistler entirely concurs.' The duel of wits developed, becoming ever more venomous on Whistler's side. 'What has Oscar in common with art? Except that he picks from our platters the plums for the pudding he peddles in the provinces.' (An alliterative riposte, perhaps, to Wilde's description of Whistler as 'a miniature Mephistopheles mocking the majority'.) The blunt, ugly truth of his attitude was saved for a private communication: 'Oscar, you really must keep outside the "radius"' – the charmed circle of the initiated.

From then on the good humour went out of the relationship; indeed, the relationship was all but dead. Wilde reviewed Whistler's book *The Gentle Art of Making Enemies* (1890) *de haut en bas*, attacking him now on his own ground: 'admirable as are Mr Whistler's fireworks on canvas, his fireworks in prose are abrupt, violent and exaggerated.' The title character in his story *The Remarkable Rocket* is a cartoon of Whistler. Meanwhile, privately and peculiarly unpleasantly, Whistler wrote to the great symbolist Stéphane Mallarmé alerting him to Wilde's Paris visit in 1891, warning him against Wilde – 'any jokester who crosses the Channel' (Mallarmé ignored the warning, and entertained Wilde enthusiastically). Their final encounter, in the last year of Wilde's life, was silent and almost hallucinatory: they entered a restaurant in Paris at exactly the same time and gazed at each other, startled. In a curious inversion of the expected sympathies, Wilde, bloated, decrepit, toothless, took pity on Whistler, noting how old and weird he looked, allowing himself one bitter joke: 'my sentence and imprisonment raised Jimmy's opinion of the English and of England. Nothing else could have done so.'

CONSTANCE WILDE (1858–98)

Constance Mary Lloyd had an Irish background: Wilde met her at a reception given by his mother in Merrion Square in 1881 when he was twenty-seven and she was twenty-three. They had taken a turn round the square, discussing poetry; she favoured Mrs Hemans and Eliza Cooke, which he did not, but they found common ground in Keats. It was after his lecture tour in Dublin two years later that they had become engaged. Nonetheless, she belongs essentially to his London life. In between the first meeting and the engagement, he had become a celebrity on both sides of the Atlantic. He was under some pressure and was becoming somewhat notorious for his epicene ways; moreover, despite his huge financial success in America, he had managed to spend himself back into penury. Everything pointed to marriage to an eligible young woman with a decent dowry. Constance fitted the bill perfectly; Lady Wilde was delighted by the match, envisaging a future in which Oscar would lead the literary life in London, while Constance read his proofs for him. (In an exquisitely improbable flight of parental fantasy, Speranza imagined him ending up as a Member of Parliament.) It was a most suitable match.

None of this is to deny that Wilde fell deeply in love with Constance. There is every evidence that he was both amorously and erotically enchanted by her: to Constance herself he wrote 'I feel your fingers in my hair, and your cheek brushing mine. The air is full of the music of your voice, my soul and body seem no longer mine, but mingled in some exquisite ecstasy with yours. I feel incomplete without you.' His description, shortly after the wedding, of his sexual pleasure with her made his friend Robert Sherard blush. Her beauty is well attested; she was also highly intelligent (she read extensively in three languages), if not intellectually adventurous. She loved him unequivocally and admiringly. 'My own darling Oscar,' she wrote to him, 'I have no power to do anything but just love you ... my whole life is yours to do with as you will.'

She was in every way an adornment to his life. The wedding (in Paddington) was a relatively restrained affair, with Constance radiant, crowned with myrtle, on her young husband's arm. From now on, the sartorial interest which had so dominated accounts of Wilde was transferred to his wife; her every gown was described in loving detail by the *Lady's Pictorial* and its sister magazines. 'He took infinite interest in her clothes (a rare quality in a husband)', as Constance's perceptive biographer Anne Clark Amor remarks, 'and loved going with her to choose more.' Not that she was a mere instrument of Oscar's will; on the contrary, she taught herself the principles of fashion and designed her own clothes, entering as fully as her essentially shy nature would allow her into the role of the wife of one of the most celebrated men in London society, presiding over dinner parties and receptions, holding the fort until he appeared (which he seems to have delayed until the last possible moment). This was no light task: the guests at her very first dinner party were the sculptor John Donoghue, John Singer Sargent, Paul Bourget (later to be a famous novelist) and a friend of Whistler's; Swinburne and Browning were in regular attendance. She never quite became a natural performer, and the relief at Oscar's arrival, both on her part and that of the guests, was palpable. Countess Anna de Brémont described 'a young woman arrayed in an exquisite Greek costume of cowslip yellow and apple-leaf green ... the whole arrangement was exceedingly becoming to the youthful, almost boyish face ... there was an air of self-consciousness and restraint about the wearer of that fantastic yet lovely costume that gave me the impression of what is called stage-fright ... imagine my surprise when she was introduced to me as the hostess.' But she was eager to learn; 'my husband and teacher', she called Wilde, and her trust in him was absolute.

The house of the Prophet of Taste had of course to be exemplary; designed by Godwin, with advice from Whistler (whose wedding present to the young couple had been a few of his Venetian Nocturnes), it was light, airy, cool. Alas, after the birth of their two children, Cyril

CONSTANCE WILDE AND HER SON CYRIL, studio of Julia Margaret Cameron, 1889

'I am going to be married to a beautiful girl called Constance Lloyd, a grave, slight, violet-eyed little Artemis, with great coils of heavy brown hair which make her flower-like head droop like a blossom, and wonderful ivory hands which draw music from the piano so sweet that the birds stop singing to listen to her', Wilde wrote to Lillie Langtry.

(1885) and Vyvyan (the following year), Wilde was spending less and less time in it. His lecturing and his independent social life frequently kept him away; more significantly, Constance's two difficult pregnancies during which she had been bloated and blotchy had killed his pleasure in her body. He quietly closed the heterosexual chapter of his life and seemed to be awaiting the opening of the homosexual. This was swiftly facilitated by the charming Canadian Ganymede who now came to stay at Tite Street as a paying guest: Robert Ross, seventeen years old and already sexually experienced. Soon Wilde moved on to other lovers; his double life had begun. Constance seemed oblivious to this development, and quietly set about pursuing her own interests. She studied fashion history at the British Museum, becoming expert in it; she started to write, pleasantly but unremarkably, for magazines; she wrote articles on the theatre. For a time she was the editor of the Rational Dress Society's *Gazette*. In 1888 the death of her grandmother – who had been a key loving substitute for her indifferent mother – provoked her to write her slim volume *There Once Was: Grandma's Stories*. Constance was keenly aware of political issues, even managing to drag Wilde to a demonstration in favour of the dock strike of 1889. Like many of her caste and generation, she was attracted to spiritualism, eventually becoming a Theosophist, and through these various strands, journalistic, political and religious, she formed part of a circle herself, one which had little to do with Wilde and his activities.

Nonetheless, she and Oscar continued their *Hello!* magazine lifestyle, attending first nights and gallery openings, engendering column inches; once Constance appeared at the Grosvenor Gallery with him dressed as an eighteenth-century highwayman. Almost without exception, however, she would retire to Tite Street at the end of the evening, while he went on to other, unnamed diversions. She was conscious of his growing notoriety, but assumed that it was due to his intellectual provocations: after the appearance of *The Picture of Dorian Gray*, she noted that 'no-one talks to us anymore'. Soon, Wilde's other life came into public view in the form of Alfred Douglas, but Constance – though she appears never to have warmed to him personally – remained unperturbed by the extraordinary amount of his time Wilde was devoting to his new friendship with the golden young lord. Once when Wilde and Douglas were holidaying together, Douglas fell ill. 'I am so sorry about Lord Alfred Douglas,' Constance wrote to Wilde, 'and I wish I was at Cromer to look after him. If you think I could be any good, do telegraph for me, because I can easily get over to you.' Oscar remained charming to her when she saw him, and was a faithful father to his boys, whom he loved tenderly and in a very modern, involved way; they were always allowed to meet company in the house, and Wilde himself would whenever possible lull them to sleep with stories, sometimes singing to them. There were happy family holidays: Oscar, reverting to his own simple childhood pleasures, swam, sailed and fished with them, proving rather adept at building sandcastles. Constance was happy to leave the boys with him when she went on a European tour; she might have been less happy had she known that Bosie and his tutor had showed up shortly after, departing after a characteristically sudden row amidst the sound of hideous screaming imprecations.

Curiously, Constance had become friendly with Bosie's long-suffering mother, Lady Queensberry, and even interceded on Bosie's behalf during one of the rare estrangements between him and Wilde. In the summer of 1894, as the relationship between the two men became ever more volatile, Bosie showed up at Worthing when Wilde was staying there with his sons; he was with a boyfriend, and demanded that Wilde should put them both up. Appalled at this intrusion of his sex life into the family home, Wilde offered to put them up at a local hotel, but then disappeared himself to stay with Bosie in Brighton. Whatever Constance made of this behaviour, she continued gallantly in the public role of Mrs Oscar Wilde: in January of 1895, as the knot of destiny tightened around Wilde, she brought out a collection of his sayings under the title of *Oscariana*; it was a big success for both of them though he loathed it. Oscar himself had stayed away from home over Christmas in order to rehearse *An Ideal Husband*; after the triumphant First Night of that, and before the impending First Night of *The Importance of Being*

Earnest, Wilde and Bosie Douglas went to Algeria in pursuit of exotic sex. While they were away, Constance had a serious and somehow symbolic accident, falling from top to bottom of the stairs of (as Anne Clark Amor ironically reminds us) the House Beautiful. Her recovery was not swift, and the spine problems that would now dog the rest of her short, troubled life, revealed themselves.

Wilde preferred to stay away from home during the build-up to the première of *The Importance of Being Earnest*; while he was in Algeria, Constance had had to resort to asking Robbie Ross (with whom she had developed a warm friendship) for his address: 'I shall very much like to know when Oscar returns.' After the first night, and Queensberry's notorious card, Constance's nightmare began in earnest. Frightened and in the dark, she learned the details of Wilde's other life from newspaper reports. After the collapse of Wilde's libel action, Robbie Ross had been despatched to break the news to her; despite her shock and grief, she urged Ross to persuade Wilde to leave the country, as she would again after the first criminal trial. Her principal concern was to keep it from the children. She was only partially successful in this: Cyril had read a newspaper placard, which someone had helpfully explained to him. He was packed off to stay with her family in Ireland, while Vyvyan remained with her.

In her bewilderment Constance wrote for reassurance to Mrs Robinson, the celebrated clairvoyant. 'What is to become of my husband who has so betrayed and deceived me and ruined the lives of my darling boys?' she asked, adding 'what a tragedy for him who is so gifted.' Before the first Crown Trial the House Beautiful and its contents were subject to auction; in one of many acts of revenge against Wilde by the British public, this was turned into another humiliation, with its exquisite furnishings sold for a song. A Whistler went for a shilling.

Throughout this devastating time, despite her rage and hurt, Constance continued to express deep love for Wilde, as she would for the rest of her life. Her advisers were divided, her brother and her friend Lady Mount-Temple knowing how profound her feeling for him was, the others baying for blood. There is a sense in all this that both of them, Constance and Wilde, were butterflies crushed on the wheel; two innocents gored by life, despite Wilde's superior worldliness. Worse was to follow for both of them. It became apparent that Constance was no more free to live her life than Wilde, now in Wandsworth Prison. She repaired with the children to Switzerland, and swiftly discovered that her married name branded her a pariah; she changed it to a family name, Holland. Nonetheless, she resisted considerable pressure to divorce Wilde; she would stick by him. There followed a series of elaborate and fraught negotiations between her representatives and Wilde's by which she sought to provide for him after he emerged from prison. The nub of most of the negotiations was her insistence on Wilde's absolute commitment to abandoning his former life – above all, Alfred Douglas. She continued to dream of a reunion: 'We women were meant to be comforters and I believe that no-one can really take my place now, nor help him as I can.' This emotion seems not to have been mutual. Wilde's affection for Constance was a thing of the past; her principal interest to him now was as a future source of income, and as the mother of his children, with whom he desperately longed to be reunited.

Meanwhile her own health was deteriorating. She had a second operation on her spine, which left her immobilised for some time. Despite this, when Wilde's mother died in February 1896 while he was in Reading Gaol, Constance returned to England from Genoa where she had moved to break the news gently to him; she found him muted and distant. It was the last time she would ever set eyes on him. After Wilde's release, he played cat and mouse with her through her representatives on the crucial matter of whether he would see Alfred Douglas or not. Their eventual reunion disgusted her: 'I have latterly (God forgive me) an absolute repulsion to him' she said of Oscar. When Wilde finally split with Bosie, he more or less demanded an allowance from Constance, which was indeed forthcoming; the rest of their relationship, conducted through third parties, consisted of unseemly haggling over money and the conditions under which it might be tendered. He sent her – but did not inscribe – a copy of *The Ballad of Reading Gaol*, which moved her deeply (she thought it 'exquisite'), as did his letters to the newspapers promoting prison reform. This was the clever and compassionate man she had loved.

Ill though she was, Constance continued to learn things: photography (she even developed her own pictures), macramé; she kept up a large correspondence, with, among others, Robbie Ross. She reserved her special contempt for Alfred Douglas, noting that he was received by high society in Rome: 'so much is it with a bourgeois nation to be of the aristocracy!' Ever mindful of her sons' need to respect Wilde, she had written Cyril a letter in which she urged him to 'try not to feel harshly about your father; remember that he is your father and he loves you. All his troubles arose from the hatred of a son for a father, and whatever he has done he has suffered bitterly for.' This was the last communication either boy ever received from her. After a third operation on her spine, she died. She was buried at Campo Santo in Genoa. On the tombstone was inscribed a verse from the last book of the Bible – for her, the Book of Life really did end with Revelations. The inscription on the tomb read, baldly, 'Constance Mary, daughter of Horace Lloyd, QC'. On being informed of her death, some five days after it happened, Wilde telegrammed to Constance's brother 'Am overwhelmed with grief. It is the most terrible tragedy.' To a friend he wrote, in a touching reversion to the sensual intimacy of the balmy early days of the marriage, 'If we had only met once, and kissed each other. It is too late. How awful life is.' When Wilde finally visited the tomb, he was moved 'with a sense of the uselessness of all regrets. Nothing could have been otherwise, and Life is a very terrible thing.' Later, the phrase 'Wife of Oscar Wilde' was added to the inscription by her family.

Just as Wilde stood in symbolic relationship to his own time, as he said, those with whom he was closely involved seem to assume symbolic, mythic outlines: Constance is the supreme example of that Wildean figure, the wronged wife. His cavalier treatment of her, bordering on callousness, reveals an aspect of the man that exists side by side with his otherwise seemingly limitless reserves of generosity and affection. Constance worshipped him; she adored him. This is not what Wilde wanted from a lover.

SIR MAX BEERBOHM (1872–1956)

Wilde first made the acquaintance of Max Beerbohm (the son of Sir Julius Beerbohm and half-brother of the actor-manager Beerbohm Tree) when Max was a schoolboy at Charterhouse. Beerbohm was from his youth a fervent admirer of Wilde the writer. His early *Ballade De La Vie Joyeuse* celebrates *The Picture of Dorian Gray*, but their friendship dates from the early nineties when Tree produced and acted in *A Woman of No Importance*.

Wilde was fascinated and perhaps a little puzzled by him: 'when you are alone with Max', he wrote to Ada Leverson, 'does he ever take off his face and reveal his mask?' Max maintained a certain detachment from Wilde the man, perhaps fearing absorption into an overpowering personal influence; he may, too, have felt a need to distance himself from the homosexual milieu in which Wilde was increasingly to be found. Because of this slight distance, he is able to offer us exceptionally clear-eyed (and clear-eared) accounts of the man, the best reports from the front we have. Wilde's voice, Max tells us, was 'a mezzo voice, uttering itself in leisurely fashion, with every variety of tone'; his talk was 'mostly monologue', but this was not his fault: 'his manners were very good: he was careful to give his fellow-guests many a conversational opening, but seldom did anyone respond with more than a few words. Nobody was willing to interrupt the music of so magnificent a virtuoso. To have heard him consoled me for not having heard Dr Johnson or Edmund Burke, Lord Brougham or Sydney Smith.' He traced the coarsening of Wilde's behaviour. Meeting him in 1893, he found himself repelled by him: 'nor have I ever seen Oscar so fatuous … of course I would rather see him free than sober.' Max followed the court case keenly, attending all three trials, and reported after hearing Wilde deliver the 'Love that Dare Not Speak its Name' speech that 'Oscar has been quite superb.' Although he made no grand gesture of solidarity with Wilde after his imprisonment, he continued to concern himself with his well-being: he helped to hatch a plan (which in the end came to nothing) to deflect attention from him at his release. His many cartoons of Wilde suggest something of the over-powering physical impact; and one particularly amusing one shows Wilde and Alfred Douglas, a huge badger charming a vole. Max was one of the recipients of *The Ballad of Reading Gaol*; a grim literary end to an association which had begun with the *Ballade De La Vie Joyeuse*.

SIR MAX BEERBOHM
Sir William
Nicholson, 1905

Tiny and perfectly formed, elegant as a tightly rolled umbrella, Max Beerbohm's huge eyes gazed with wry melancholy on the world's absurdities even as a very young man ('Gods have bestowed on Max', Wilde observed, 'the gift of eternal old age').

AUBREY BEARDSLEY (1872–98)

Oscar Wilde always maintained that he had invented Aubrey Beardsley. This was as idle a claim as his boast that he had invented the green carnation (it came from Goodyear's in the Royal Arcade: 'they grow them there'). In fact, Beardsley had very much invented himself: a figure unique in English art, without precedent and with all too many imitators. It is true that Wilde had encouraged him from a very early age: they met at Edward Burne-Jones's house when Beardsley was eighteen, and quickly became friends. Their only professional association was over the English edition of *Salomé*, and it soured the relationship. Beardsley had done a drawing of Salomé holding the head of John the Baptist for the April 1893 edition of *The Studio*; Wilde liked it and commissioned him to provide the illustrations for his play. In this he was much encouraged by Robbie Ross, whose enthusiasm for Beardsley's work was absolute: of the *Salomé* illustrations he said, 'In the whole range of art there is nothing like them', and he was no doubt right. Their extreme stylisation, presenting a world of grotesques, by turns – sometimes simultaneously – etiolated and bloated, in an exquisite black and white line, combining, as Ellmann says, the manner of the eighteenth century with *fin-de-siècle* decadence, presents a vividly creative response to Wilde's biblical world without actually embodying it. It is as if a radical director and designer had re-imagined Wilde's play. Wilde was taken aback by the audacity and strangeness of the pictures,

AUBREY BEARDSLEY, Frederick Evans, 1894

Wilde had not been altogether complimentary about Beardsley's personal appearance ('his face like a silver hatchet, with green-grass hair') and their friendship soured into catty exchanges in which Wilde showed that he could dish it out *de haut en bas* with the best of them: 'dear Aubrey is almost too Parisian – he can never forget that he has been to Dieppe – once.'

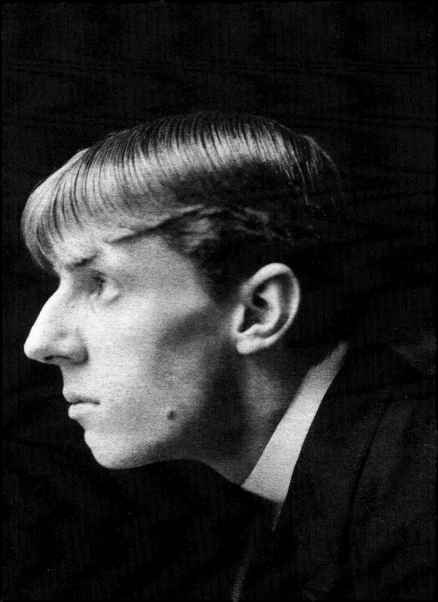

so far from the richly costumed, bedizened images he had in mind. What shook him most severely was the fact that he himself unmistakably appeared in a number of the illustrations, unkindly caricatured as puffily fat, effeminate, evil, in jester's cap and bells, one of the friendliest of the public representations by which he had been shadowed from early manhood. Nonetheless, he could scarcely doubt the power and sensational originality of Beardsley's work. The artist, already in the grip of the tuberculosis that would kill him before the decade was out, was demonstrating some of the venomous behaviour which became increasingly characteristic of him.

An 1893 Beardsley cartoon of Wilde at the time of *Salomé* shows him surrounded by books – not only Josephus and the Bible, which is perfectly respectable, but also Gautier, Swinburne and Flaubert's *Trois Contes*, which flags the sensitive subject of plagiarism. Finally, ultimately insultingly, are found *French Verbs at a Glance, Ahn's First Course* and a French dictionary. Beardsley's attitude to Wilde, though, is also a striking example of the positive repulsion which a number of people felt for Wilde, both physically and personally. 'He is a great white caterpillar', famously remarked Lady Colin Campbell.

After Wilde's release from prison, he found himself at dinner with Beardsley, who was very cordial to him; soon after Wilde invited him to supper in Berneval, in Normandy, where he lived for a while, but Beardsley never showed up. 'A boy like that whom I made!' wrote Wilde. 'No, it was too *lâche* [cowardly] of Aubrey.' Later, he visited Beardsley in Boulogne, but Beardsley asked him not to do so again. Soon after, racked with disease, he died. Wilde was moved to write to a correspondent: 'there is something macabre and tragic in the fact that one who added a new terror to life should have died at the age of a flower.'

SIR GEORGE ALEXANDER (1858–1918) AND SIR HERBERT BEERBOHM TREE (1852–1917)

The consummately elegant actor George Alexander, an urbane and intelligent, though not an especially imaginative, man, took the St James's Theatre in 1890 to provide a home for new British plays. One of the first approaches he made was to Wilde, who replied by sending him his early and unsuccessful *Duchess of Padua*, which Alexander turned down on the perhaps tactful grounds that the scenery would be too expensive. Instead he offered him a hundred pounds to write an original play set in the present time. Despite the failure of his previous work for the theatre, there was no question that Wilde had an extraordinary, even an exceptional, ability for fabricating dramatic narratives; the dialogue in his books too was brilliant and speakable, hardly surprising in the man who was universally conceded to be the supreme talker of his day. It was a happy day, then, when Alexander persuaded him to write about his own world. Naturally Wilde dawdled over the commission, as he did over most obligatory tasks, but in the autumn of 1891 he presented Alexander with *Lady Windermere's Fan*. Like Mahler's symphonies, Wilde's plays were written on holiday; unlike Mahler's symphonies, they generally took no more than three or four weeks to finish. Alexander was delighted with the play, which provided him with an excellent role, that of Lady Windermere. He immediately offered Wilde £1,000 outright for it, which Wilde immediately declined, preferring to take royalties; in the event the play earned him £7,000 on its first run.

Wilde showed no undue humility about what was virtually a new departure for him. He attended rehearsals, offering his advice at every turn. He was not as enthusiastic about taking advice, however, and made two major changes to the play only after the first night had proved Alexander and the actors right; this what Alexander called his 'damned Irish obstinacy'. Wilde was at the zenith of his belief in the absolute and unquestioned sovereignty of the artist – the literary artist, that is; he was unwilling to give the producer or the actors that status. 'The actor's aim', he wrote in a letter to the *Daily Telegraph*, 'is or should be to convert his own accidental personality into the real and essential personality of the character he is called upon to personate.' Sounding strikingly like the revolutionary theatre artist Edward Gordon Craig at his most radical, he continued: 'the personality of the actor is often a source of danger in the perfect presentation of a work of art. It may distort. It may lead astray. It may be a discord in a tone or symphony. For anybody can act. Most people in England do nothing else.' Of Alexander himself, Wilde said: 'he does not act: he behaves', presumably a compliment. His lightness of touch in these matters had not left him, however. His disquisition on acting ended with a paean to puppets. He had seen *The Tempest* in Paris performed by marionettes: 'Miranda was the mirage of Miranda, because an artist had made her … it was a delightful performance, and I remember it with delight, though Miranda took no notice of the flowers I sent her after the curtain fell.' He was equally scornful of his fellow dramatists: 'There are three rules for writing plays. The first rule is not to write like Henry Arthur Jones; the second and third rules are the same.' Later he made another somewhat surprising statement about the art form he had adopted: 'If we are to have a real drama in England, I feel sure it will only be on condition that we wean ourselves from the trammelling conventions which have always been a peril to the theatre. I do not think it makes the smallest difference what a play is if an actor has genius and power.' To this, he added a gratuitous snub to the audience: 'Nor do I consider the British public to be of the slightest importance'.

Needless to say, Wilde enjoyed the razzmatazz of the theatre; ex-King of Publicity that he was, he even invented a new promotional idea, arranging for all the young men in the audience of the First Night of *Lady Windermere's Fan* to wear the new green carnations; a young man on stage would wear one too. '"This will be some secret symbol," the audience will say, "what on earth can it mean?" And what does it mean? Nothing whatever, but that it's just what nobody will guess.'

He could have given tutorials to any modern advertising agency. *Lady Windermere's Fan* was a sensational success; it was immediately recognised by many people that a new voice in the theatre had made itself heard. Or perhaps an old voice, the voice of the witty comedy of a century before. The critical response was somewhat brittle, finding the wit formulaic and the plotting melodramatic, but the audience in the theatre was in no doubt: this worked. The author took to the stage to acknowledge the acclaim: 'Ladies and gentlemen,' he said with his languid inflections, as reported to Hesketh Pearson by George Alexander, 'I have enjoyed this evening *immensely*. The actors have given us a *charming* rendition of a *delightful* play, and your appreciation has been *most* intelligent. I congratulate you on the *great* success of your performance, which persuades me you think *almost* as highly of the play as I do myself.' He was smoking a cigarette, a cause of scandal among the critical fraternity, but he had an answer for them: 'Ladies and gentlemen, it's perhaps not very proper to smoke in front of you … but it's not very proper to disturb me when I am smoking.'

While *Lady Windermere's Fan* was running, a burlesque skit on Wilde called *The Poet and the Puppets* (after his *Daily Telegraph* piece) was staged, written and performed by an eccentric character actor and sketch writer named Charles Brookfield; the brilliant comedian Charles Hawtrey starred, unmistakably attired as Wilde. It was as if the ten years since *Patience* had never been – except of course that now Wilde was a major figure at the centre of his world; it was upon his fame that the show rode. With *Patience* he had been a peripheral one whose celebrity was created by the show. The significance of *The Poet and the Puppets* is that it is symptomatic of a certain rising irritation with Wilde. 'It appears to me that from the first we have gone out of our way to convert Mr Wilde into a personage, and that he quite appreciates the advantage of the position and does not mean to let us off … Mr Charles Hawtrey makes up wonderfully as Mr Wilde, and I daresay reproduces his manner and attitude very well also; I can say no more than that, for

I have not thought Mr Wilde of sufficient importance to observe him very closely. I fancy that the bulk of our British 40 millions are much in the same position.' But nothing could stop the success of Wilde's play.

From now on his fortune was made, his literary immortality ensured; he had found his ideal métier. Plays followed one another in swift succession. *A Woman of No Importance* (1893) was written for Beerbohm Tree, who was the highly successful manager of the Theatre Royal Haymarket. Alexander's senior by some years, he was an altogether more expansive and exotic personality than the younger man. Where Alexander was somewhat anxious about Wilde's overwhelming personality, 'the Chief,' as he was known, was every bit as commanding as the dramatist. 'How are you?' his half-brother Max had once asked him. 'I?', said Tree, 'I? Oh, I'm *radiant.*' And he generally was. Wilde felt him quite unsuitable for the role of Lord Illingworth ('you might play Herod in my *Salomé*', he said), but succumbed, as most people did, to his amiable persuasions. Nonetheless he warned Tree: 'you had better forget that you have ever acted at all … [Illingworth] is like no one who has existed before … indeed, if you can bear the truth, he is MYSELF.' Taking this persiflage to heart, Tree began to model himself on Wilde. 'Ah, every day Herbert becomes *de plus en plus Oscarisé*', observed the dramatist, 'it is a wonderful case of Nature imitating Art.' He achieved an exceptional success in the part; it became one of his favourite roles. The play, too, was highly successful; the reviewers noted that Wilde had taken a step forward with it. At the curtain call there were boos among the cheers; Wilde (this time wearing lilies in his lapel in place of the carnation) puckishly observed: 'Ladies and Gentlemen, Mr Oscar Wilde, I regret to say, is not in the house.' The Prince of Wales came to the play on the second night and insisted that Wilde change nothing in the play.

The third of Wilde's modern plays, *An Ideal Husband* (1895), was produced by Tree, but there was no role for him in it; Lewis Waller and Charles Hawtrey, the best romantic actor and the finest high comedian, respectively, of their day, played, respectively, Sir Robert Chiltern and Lord Goring, while Charles Brookfield, author of *The Poet and the Puppets*,

SIR HERBERT BEERBOHM TREE, Harrington Mann, n.d.

Wilde's association with Tree was a happy one, and they became friendly. 'I shall always regard you as the best critic of my plays', said Wilde. 'But', replied Tree, 'I have never criticised your plays.' 'That is why'.

played Goring's valet, on the grounds that the fewer of Wilde's lines he had to say, the better. Hawtrey and Brookfield, united in their loathing of the dramatist, must have engendered a certain amount of tension during rehearsals, but if so Wilde was oblivious to it, perhaps not surprisingly, considering the growing drama in his private life. He insisted on rehearsing on Christmas Day, another deeply unpopular move (especially since he himself showed up an hour late). But the smell of success was in the air, and actors will put up with a great deal when that is the case. This time, it was the first night rather than the second which the Prince of Wales graced with his presence; also in the audience were the Prime Minister, the future Prime Minister Arthur Balfour, and Joseph Chamberlain the leader of the Liberal Unionists. It is impossible to think of another British dramatist who could, then or now, have commanded such a glittering première; the date was 3 January 1895. A mere five months later the hero of that occasion was standing in the dock of the Old Bailey to hear himself condemned to two years' hard labour. The reviews for the play were respectful; Shaw acclaimed Wilde as 'our only thorough playwright. He plays with everything, with wit, with philosophy, with drama, with actors and with audience, with the whole theatre ...' Critics, Shaw said, 'laugh angrily at Wilde's epigrams'. In an interview (with Robbie Ross) Wilde allowed himself one of his sallies against them. 'Real critics! Ah, how perfectly charming they would be! I am always waiting for their arrival. An inaudible school would be nice ...' There was no first night speech from the author; he had, said Tree, left the theatre. This was not true. Perhaps he was nervous; perhaps he could think of nothing new to say. Certainly he had much to preoccupy him as Queensberry became more and more aggressive. Supper after the show was a quiet affair between Tree, his brother Max, Wilde and Bosie Douglas.

There was to be one more glittering First Night, one more dazzling triumph, and it was the greatest of them all, perhaps the greatest of the nineteenth century. *The Importance of Being Earnest*, most perfectly absurd of love intrigues, was scheduled to have its first night on Valentine's Day, 14 February, exactly a fortnight after the première of

An Ideal Husband. Again, there seems to be no precedent and has certainly been no sequel in theatrical history to this rapid succession of masterpieces. On this occasion the play was back in the hands of George Alexander, who had initially turned it down, as being unsuitable to his particular gifts; Wilde had suspected as much: 'you are a romantic actor', he had told him. Wilde, who had knocked the play off with even greater fluency than usual, was generally rather worried, in fact, that the whole thing might be too frivolous, so he sent Alexander an outline for a play in which, he said, '*I want the sheer passion of love to dominate everything.* No morbid self-sacrifice. No renunciation – a sheer flame of love between a man and a woman.' This is a striking new development in Wilde's art, heading as he was towards his own nemesis in the name of just such a passion.

The fluency with which he wrote *The Importance of Being Earnest* led to an *embarras de richesses*: Alexander became convinced that its four acts were one too many. As an author, Wilde was far from enthusiastic about rewriting, much less about cuts, but on this occasion he allowed himself to be persuaded, with a more or less good grace, to cut a substantial scene featuring the solicitor Gribsby and turn Acts II and III into a single act. He pretended to be put out: 'The scene that you feel is superfluous cost me terrible exhausting labour and heart-rending nerve-wracking strain', he told Alexander. 'You may not believe me, but I assure you on my honour that it must have taken fully five minutes to write.' He was more than usually amenable, on account, perhaps, of what he felt to be the frivolous nature of the piece, or perhaps because of the ever madder pace of his private affairs, threatened on the one hand by Queensberry's increasing activity, on the other by his own escalating sexual indulgence. During most of the rehearsal period he was with Bosie in Algeria, where they met the novelist André Gide, who has left a lurid but not unconvincing account of their sexual adventures: at one point, Bosie fell in love with a twelve-year-old Arab boy and decamped to pursue him, while Wilde seemed to be engaging in voyeuristic pleasures, prodding Gide into acceptance of his own pederastic inclinations.

They returned in time for the dress rehearsal, after which Wilde told Alexander, 'Well, Alec, I suppose we must start rehearsals for the play on Monday.' Asked by a critic whether the play would be a success, he replied, 'The play *is* a success. The only question is whether the first night's audience will be one.' It was. Few audiences have behaved better; they laughed and laughed; at the end they cheered. Wilde himself was in the wings throughout, painfully conscious of Queensberry outside the theatre, circling it like a shark. One of the actors asked him if he'd take a call. 'No,' he said, 'I took one last night at the Haymarket, and one feels so much like a *German band*.'

The reviews were exceptionally warm, the critics feeling – like most subsequent theatregoers – that he had 'found himself', as, in the words of A.B. Walkley, 'an artist in sheer nonsense'. Shaw was disappointed because he wasn't moved – or so he said; what he probably meant was that he wasn't moved to *thought*.

Interestingly, Wilde was somewhat disparaging about the huge success of the play. No doubt his mind was set on the play about *sheer passion*. He had told Gide that 'my special duty is to plunge madly into amusement … No, not happiness … pleasure. One must always set one's heart upon the most tragic.' Meanwhile, Wilde had received Queensberry's provocative card and had filed his action for criminal libel against him. Two days before the trial he took Bosie and Constance to see the play; the three of them sat in a box together. Bosie was tense, Constance tearful, but Wilde, apparently oblivious, went backstage to

GEORGE ALEXANDER, AS JOHN WORTHING, WITH ALLAN AYNESWORTH, AS ALGERNON MONCRIEFFE in *The Importance of Being Earnest*, St James's Theatre, 1895
Alfred Ellis, 1895

Wilde went to see Alexander, who had given the comic performance of his lifetime by playing his part (Jack) entirely straight, and congratulated him: 'Charming, quite charming. And do you know, from time to time I was reminded of a play I once wrote myself called *The Importance of Being Earnest*', which was both funny and to some extent true, in view of the unusual amount that had been cut from it.

see George Alexander, who urgently advised him to drop the case and go abroad. 'I have just been abroad', said Wilde. 'One can't keep going abroad, unless one is a missionary, or, what comes to the same thing, a commercial traveller.' He assured Alexander that all would be well; the palmist Mrs Robinson had told him so. 'Do you believe in palmists?' asked the astonished Alexander. 'Always … when they prophesy nice things.' 'When do they ever prophesy anything else?' 'Never. If they did, no one would believe in them, and the poor creatures must earn a living somehow.' 'Oh, you're impossible!' cried Alexander, not entirely admiringly. 'No, not impossible, my dear fellow. Improbable … yes … I grant you improbable.'

When Wilde's case collapsed, Alexander immediately withdrew Wilde's name from the playbills: 'a peculiarly Victorian form of humbug', as Pearson, an admirer of Alexander's, succinctly put it. The play ran until 8 May, while Wilde was in Holloway Gaol, awaiting trial. His effacement from respectable society had begun. Alexander and Waller, meanwhile, refused to stand bail for him.

Wilde's days as a dramatist were over. Before the trial he had been toying with writing a story that he had often told. He called it *La Sainte Courtisane*. Asked how it was proceeding, he answered, 'She keeps saying wonderful things, but the Anchorite always remains mute. I admit her words are quite unanswerable. I think I shall have to indicate his replies by stars or asterisks.' He gave an almost complete manuscript to Ada Leverson before the trial; she restored it to him in 1897, when he emerged from prison, whereupon he left it in a cab. 'A very proper place for it', he observed. Otherwise, he tried to interest various producers in the outline of the play about *sheer passion* which he had sent George Alexander. A number of them gave him advances to write it; Frank Harris offered actually to write it for him, and did, but it is a poor thing which bears little trace of Wilde's wit, style or *sheer passion*.

Wilde had a slightly uneasy relationship to the theatre of his time. However humorously tilted, his attitude was very much that of the artist condescending to a grubby and a compromised medium. There was a certain *folie de grandeur* about his manner (after *An Ideal Husband* opened, for instance, he remarked: 'It is only in the last few years that the dramatic critic has had the opportunity of seeing plays written by anyone who has a mastery of style') which invited comeuppance; when he received it in such devastatingly disproportionate terms, there were many who rejoiced, though many others were appalled. Few came to his aid. One, Charles Brookfield, who had guyed him in *The Poet and the Puppets*, actively hastened his ruin by putting Queensberry in touch with the female prostitutes who were able to connect him with the male brothels which finally yielded the incriminating evidence. (By an exquisite turn of fate which Wilde alas never lived to witness, Brookfield later became the Censor of Plays.)

George Alexander, whose career both as actor and as manager had gained so much from Wilde, behaved shabbily, not only in the matter of the playbills, but also in snapping up the rights in *An Ideal Husband* and *A Woman of No Importance* for a song at the bankruptcy proceedings; even worse, passing Wilde in France, he cycled swiftly on, his face a smirking mask. Later, he partially redeemed himself by approaching Wilde and voluntarily offering him a small royalty in his plays (which were being revived as early as 1898); he bequeathed the rights to Wilde's sons. Tree sent Wilde some money in the last year of his life, with the words: 'No one did such distinguished work as you ... I do most sincerely hope that your splendid talents may shine forth again.' There were emotional scenes with Sarah Bernhardt; and Ellen Terry, who had delivered flowers with a supportive message to his house after the collapse, had, with Aimée Lowther, bumped into him in Paris in 1899 peering wistfully into the window of a pastry shop. They invited him for supper, when he held forth as expansively as ever.

From the rest of the profession that had so benefited from his brief, dazzling contribution to their lives, there was a not very edifying silence.

GAY
FRIENDS

ROBERT 'ROBBIE' ROSS (1869–1918)

Oscar Wilde's name has become synonymous with homosexuality to such a degree that it is something of a shock to realise that his first experience of that sort seems not to have occurred until he was thirty-two years old, so that the homosexual part of his life lasted no more than twelve years. His introduction to it was almost certainly effected by the seventeen-year-old Robert Ross, at Wilde's house in Tite Street, where Ross was staying as a paying guest. His long delayed acceptance of what was obvious to so many is a little baffling. It is a curiosity of Wilde's life that he seemed for at least ten years before succumbing to his nature to have been rehearsing the role of a homosexual. This was quite a complicated game, psychologically speaking: pretending to be something that he was. Occasionally, he opened the door a crack on his desires: 'If you'd have been a boy', he told the gamine young actress Aimée Lowther, 'you'd have wrecked my life'. His poems, especially on Greek themes, sometimes hint at homosexual interest; now and then they come right out with it. Why did he wait so long? He certainly knew a number of homosexuals. Perhaps he simply hadn't met the right man. He told a friend at the end of his life that once, shopping with his wife, he had seen the male prostitutes hanging around Piccadilly Circus (as they still do today) and 'something clutched at my heart like ice'. Although he was later to take great delight in the company and services of boy prostitutes, both in England and in Europe, he may, in his mid-thirties, have feared the scandal and recoiled from the sordidness of the transaction. What he needed was someone to take the lead, to initiate him. By a paradox which is perfectly Wildean, the initiator would ideally be a boy, beautiful, lithe, exquisite. So when the slim, charming, sexually experienced Robbie Ross took Wilde's pose of homosexuality at face value, it must have been an immense relief to him. There is no sense whatever of Wilde as

ROBERT BALDWIN ROSS, Elliott & Fry, *c*.1914

'St Robert of Phillimore', Wilde dubbed Ross from prison, after his address in Kensington, 'lover and martyr ... a saint known for his extraordinary power, not in resisting, but in supplying temptations to others. This he did in the solitude of great cities, to which he retired at the comparatively early age of eight.'

a sexual predator; in many ways, his relationship to both life and love was passive (though not necessarily sexually, not, that is, in the technical sense). Sex was dalliance, to him, romance; it was bound up with flirtation and ravishment of the senses, not with the intensity of orgasm. Thus, once Constance's boyishly slight figure and perfect complexion had been marred by her two difficult pregnancies, romance disappeared, and there was nothing left. Robbie arrived at exactly the right time.

As well as being sexually at ease, he was a witty and responsive companion and Wilde was enchanted by him. He was scarcely to know then that Robbie would prove to be the mainstay of his life, the supervisor of his deathbed, the arranger of his posterity. In his last years Wilde said that he had had three marriages, one to a woman, and two to men; it is generally assumed that by the latter he meant Robbie Ross and Bosie Douglas. Yet his love for Robbie was a very different thing from what he felt for Bosie; Robbie was not the man to inspire a mad passion. Robbie was for friendship. His biographer has dubbed him 'The Friend of Friends', and certainly his friendship for Wilde was an exemplary thing, but it was a relationship like those so characteristic of gay people, in which a brief sexual or romantic association modulates into a deep and permanent devotion.

Canadian by nationality, Ross had been born in Tours (and, indeed, on tour), in 1869; his father died in 1871, and, at his father's dying behest, the family had moved to London. In the early 1880s they lived in South Kensington, in Onslow Square. Ross claimed – his biographer is sceptical – that as a lad he had bumped into Carlyle, hairy and ancient, who had instructed him to call himself Robbie, in the proper Scots manner. He says of his parents – and this is a fair example of the charming, slightly whimsical style which had endeared him to Wilde – 'They revered Mr Carlyle as a Scotsman who shed lustre on the race inhabiting the northern part of the island. They clothed their minds in intellectual kilts; and I, their child, was also clothed for a brief period in that revolting garment which led to an early, premature sympathy for the perpetrators of the Glencoe massacre.' His education was vague, being mainly in the hands of a private tutor with whom he toured Europe; this may be the source of his early sexual experience. Certainly, his academic prowess was in need of a boost if he was to get into King's Cambridge, and he duly attended a crammer in London; it was during this period that he lodged with the Wildes. He went up to Cambridge in October 1888, writing for, among other magazines, the newly founded *Granta*, but his time there was not happy: he fell foul of a gang of hearties, who threw him into the fountain, after which he contracted pneumonia; recovering, he then fell prey to measles. He quit King's after a year, without a degree. At around this time, he and Wilde had discussed the story that became *The Portrait of Mr W H*, in which Wilde proposes that the sonnets were addressed to a boy player in Shakespeare's theatre, Willie Hughes; Wilde told Robbie that the book – among his favourites – was as much Robbie's as it was his. It is the most substantial memorial of their love affair. By this time, Wilde had moved on to another young man, the poet John Gray, who loved Wilde with intense devotion (never Wilde's favourite emotion), but this affair too was swept aside by the all-conquering figure of Lord Alfred Douglas.

Meanwhile for Robbie there was a crisis at home – not the first, nor the last – about his unabashed (though discreet) homosexuality, which he stubbornly refused to renounce. As a punishment he was sent to Scotland to work for the *Scots Observer*, then started to work for the Society of Authors, swiftly becoming its deputy editor. With his friend More Adey he edited *Melmoth The Wanderer*, by Wilde's great-uncle Charles Maturin. He was beginning to find his place – as a diligent, tasteful, witty stage manager of other men's work and talents. He remained part of Wilde's life, staying with him in Goring while Oscar wrote *Lady Windermere's Fan*, attending the First Night with a green carnation in his buttonhole, along with a number of other young men, similarly embellished. Then, in 1893, disaster struck: he was implicated in a potential scandal concerning a sixteen-year-old boy he had picked up at a railway station and whom he had passed on to Alfred Douglas, who had in turn passed him on to Wilde. All three were saved by the shrewd advice of the solicitor George Lewis, who pointed out to the aggrieved parent that if he went to law, his son would have to appear in court as well; the case was dropped. Robbie's family insisted that he leave the country: 'the disgrace of the family, a social outcast, a son and a brother unfit for society of any kind'. He withdrew to Davos (where, incorrigible, he lectured on Greek love), supposedly for two years, but he managed to sneak back early, just in time in fact, to take on the role for which history now knows him, that of Wilde's Faithful Friend. He was the first person to whom Wilde – instantly and correctly – turned after receiving the Marquess of Queensberry's famous abusive card: 'I don't know what to do. If you could come here at 11.30, please do so tonight. I mar your life by trespassing ever on your love and kindness.' Robbie had already (perhaps unfortunately) introduced Wilde to the solicitor Travis Humphreys, who proved to be more than a little out of his depth during the subsequent events; from now on he devoted himself full time to helping Wilde – in so far as Wilde would allow himself to be helped. Ross accompanied him after the collapse of the first trial, cashing a cheque for £200 for him as he made his way to the Cadogan Hotel; it was he who was entrusted with the awful mission of breaking the news to Constance. No one was better suited for the task; his relationship with her had continued warm since the early days in Tite Street. In the summer of 1892 Constance had invited Robbie to join them on holiday in Babbacombe 'for as long as he liked'. The advent of Alfred Douglas into Wilde's life had pushed them closer together, two discarded lovers. At least Robbie knew that this is what had happened to him; Constance remained in the dark, about both Wilde and Ross. Their mutual enthusiasm for the Roman Catholic Church increased the bond: Ross, like so many homosexuals of the period, was a convert. At one point, Constance sent him a rosary; he sent her in return a manual on the correct use of one. At Christmas 1894, while Wilde was absent from home rehearsing *An Ideal Husband*, Ross sent flowers to Constance and presents for the boys. She found his company, she said, 'delightful'.

When Ross arrived to break the news of the collapse of the trial, Constance begged him to urge Wilde to leave the country, which he did, but to no avail. After Wilde was arrested Ross went back to Tite Street to pack a bag for Wilde; he and the butler Arthur had to break down the bedroom door, which had been locked. He took the bag to Bow Street, where Wilde was being held. He then returned to Tite Street, removing any manuscripts and letters he could find. By now he was in a state of terror: he was, of course, at grave risk of arrest himself. He returned to his mother's house and collapsed. She begged him to leave the country; he finally agreed to do so when she promised to commit £500 for Wilde's defence. He read of Wilde's trial in Calais; the sentence was delivered, as Ross's biographer points out, on 25 May 1895, Ross's twenty-sixth birthday. He crept back into the country in time to perform an act of great symbolic importance: he managed to station himself within Wilde's eye-line when he was taken from prison to the bankruptcy court. As Wilde passed, Ross gravely raised his hat to him. 'Men have gone to heaven for smaller things than that', Wilde wrote in *De Profundis*. Ross thenceforward devoted himself to trying to secure Wilde's financial future, arranging subscriptions, negotiating with Constance. Throughout the sometimes rebarbative exchanges between the representatives of Wilde and those of Constance, her trust for Ross scarcely wavered; between them they hammered out a series of conditions which Wilde did his best not to meet. Wilde meanwhile appointed Ross his literary executor as well as his chancellor of exchequer; his demands became increasingly querulous, occasionally erupting into denunciations of Ross's always well-meant but occasionally amateur efforts on his behalf. Three times, Ross visited him in prison, and each time was shaken by the change that had overcome him; for a while he doubted whether Wilde would survive. Ross himself, frail of health from childhood, began to suffer under the strain.

After Wilde's release, Ross was at Dieppe to greet him. Wilde – 'with that odd elephantine gait which I have never seen in anyone else' – placed in his hands the manuscript of *De Profundis*: 'this, my dear Bobbie, is the great manuscript of which you know.' For the remaining three years of Wilde's life, Ross assumed the frequently thankless role of container of his extravagance, fruitlessly urging on him discretion, both financial and sexual; discretion was the core of Robbie's being, his religion, but Wilde was not for conversion. (As far as formal religion went, Ross kept up a gentle flow of propaganda on behalf of the Church of Rome, which did not fall on deaf ears, though Wilde remained teasingly averse to actual commitment.) His attempts at encouraging Wilde to write were doomed; all too often he found himself in the role of the scold, prefect of Wilde's profligacy as he drank and dallied his way to the grave. 'With best love, dear horrid, irritating Robbie',

Wilde signed off one letter. There were times when Ross refused to play the role – he was particularly incensed when Wilde had a reconciliation with Alfred Douglas, not only slapping his loyal friends in the face, but also destroying the careful rapprochement Ross had constructed with Constance. Invariably, inevitably, he returned to the task. It was his lot in life. He discharged his function as guardian of Wilde's literary reputation quite impeccably, arranging for the gradual reappearance of the works some of them under the unlikely banner of Leonard Smithers, specialist in 'adult' literature, whose vulgarity appalled him. Robbie had his reward, however: *The Importance of Being Earnest*, when it appeared in a new edition in 1898, bore the dedication 'To Robert Baldwin Ross/in appreciation/in affection'. Who could ask for more?

When Constance died, in 1898, he was considerably more affected by it than Wilde had been. By the end of her life she had formed a strong attachment to him: 'I have never seen anything in a man like him … at first, as you know was the case with me, one scarcely believes it. But now I not only believe but admire and am astounded by it.' He was deeply upset by Beardsley's death shortly after. Now he had to deal with Wilde's. While Wilde was dying ('beyond my means') he had murmured, 'Robbie, dear Robbie, when the Last Trumpet sounds, and we are couched in our porphyry tombs, I shall turn to you and whisper to you, "Robbie, dear Robbie, let us pretend we do not hear it."' Wilde appeared to be in a relatively stable condition, so Ross went off for a brief sojourn to the South of France, but then hastened back when Reggie Turner sent urgent telegrams indicating that the end was near. By the time Ross returned, Wilde was in a coma. He never spoke again. Ross brought in a priest to admit Wilde, despite his lack of consciousness, into the Roman communion. Mahaffy was finally defeated. Depending on your point of view, this may have been the greatest of all the services Robbie Ross rendered him.

He and Reggie Turner (and Jean Dupoirier, in whose Hotel d'Alsace in the rue des Beaux-Arts Wilde was living) were present for the death itself, an event of almost primitive physicality, in which a monstrously extended death rattle was succeeded by an explosion of fluids from ears, mouth, rectum. After the death Ross sent telegrams to Frank Harris and Bosie Douglas, who immediately came for the modest funeral – sixth class. Wilde was buried at Bagneux in Paris with a simple tombstone (inscribed with a quotation, of all fitting books of the Bible, from Job); about twenty people were present. Ross continued about his work of rehabilitation; among his most important acts was the publication of *De Profundis*, in expurgated form, in 1905. In 1912 the Epstein tomb was installed in Père Lachaise; Robbie expressed a desire in his will to be buried in it. His death happened much earlier than could possibly have been imagined, in 1918, when he was not yet fifty. The puckish boy who had so fatefully arrived at Tite Street to relieve Oscar of his heterosexuality had become a bald, trim, prematurely aged figure, anxious and exhausted. Alfred Douglas was largely responsible for this, having pursued him with his own special brand of hysterical vindictiveness in a series of magazine articles and books, calling him 'probably the foulest and filthiest being drawing the breath of life'. In a ghostly replay of Wilde's trial, Ross took Bosie to court for libel, but finally withdrew the case, for fear that details of his own private life would emerge. In 1918 the crazed far right-wing MP Noël Pemberton-Billing, a crony of Douglas's, was taken to court for libelling Maud Allan, who had given the British premiere of *Salomé*; that trial became a posthumous re-trial of Wilde, and a public pillorying of Ross. Ross sank into quiet despair, succumbing later that year with hardly a murmur to heart failure, a discreet end to a discreet life.

His obituary in *The Times* observed that 'it was his foible to pretend to be a trifler in all things and to gibe at the greatest reputation; but he knew more and did more than many solemn people and, in acts of kindness, he was always in earnest.' That perhaps unconscious allusion to the play of which he was the dedicatee was yet another acknowledgement that his life, productive in so many other ways, had nonetheless been distinguished above all by his role in Oscar Wilde's life. With this historical verdict, Robbie Ross would have been perfectly happy, though in what is surely one of the saddest and most unsparing of all self-judgements, he confided in Frank Harris, towards the end of his life, that he did not believe that Wilde had ever really liked him. In the light of that, his devotion seems all the more noble. Certainly, unlike many of Wilde's associates, he had no desire for public recognition. His place was backstage; his flamboyance, wit and occasional asperity were strictly reserved for private consumption. Posterity has decided to push him gently into the spotlight, however, and he has received the posthumous gratitude of generations of Oscarians as the epitome and paragon of unselfish friendship. There is something profoundly fitting in his ashes being interred with Wilde's in Père Lachaise, though even in this, Robbie's reward was some time in coming: it finally happened in 1950, half a century after Wilde's death, more than thirty years after his own.

LORD ALFRED DOUGLAS (1870–1945)

Much has been made of the fact that when Wilde created the character of Dorian Gray, he seemed to be predicting the arrival in his life of Alfred Douglas (it is faintly ironic, then, that Dorian was named after Wilde's current paramour, John Gray, as a gesture of love). The physical description is not especially accurate, but the account of the emotional impact is uncanny: 'I had come face to face with someone whose mere personality was so fascinating that, if I allowed it to do so, it would absorb my whole nature, my whole soul, my very art itself', says the painter Basil Hallward in the novel. 'I had a strange feeling that fate had in store for me exquisite joys and infinite sorrows.' In fact, their first encounter did not produce quite the *coup de foudre* that so devastated Hallward; they were introduced by Lionel Johnson, another undergraduate poet whom Wilde had encountered in the course of his systematic courtship of Oxford's *jeunesse dorée* in the late eighties ('he discoursed with infinite flippancy of everyone; lauded The Dial; laughed at Pater and consumed all my cigarettes', said Johnson, 'I am in love with him'). Wilde was immediately and predictably charmed by Bosie's appearance and personality, but the fuse was a slow one to ignite. It took a little while, perhaps, for Wilde to realise how intensely he needed to have his life disrupted, and how perfectly Bosie would accomplish this. To begin with there were pleasant flirtatious communications, an exchange of slim volumes; Wilde invited him to the First Night of *Lady Windermere's Fan*. In that same year, 1892, Bosie came to him with a blackmail threat he had received. Wilde helped him financially and arranged for his solicitor to help. It seems that this extremely intimate negotiation, which nothing in their previous relationship would have seemed to justify, led to a physical consummation, which in turn led to an emotional engagement on both their parts which would dominate both their lives to the very end.

It also seems that that is exactly what Bosie wanted. His approach to Wilde was a complex ploy: he was saying explicitly 'we're queer and we're in this together'; he deliberately put himself into Wilde's debt. It is the move of someone who wants a close relationship of one sort or another. As far as the sexual event goes, it was apparently not a great success. Wilde was by no means Bosie's *beau idéal*: he favoured youths, preferably of the working class. Bosie's sexual career at Winchester had evidently been spectacular: his schoolfellow Sir Edmund Backhouse, the 'Hermit of Peking', in his autobiography recalled many joyful couplings with him. When Bosie went up to Oxford, he immediately became, in his most recent biographer's words, 'the most famous homosexual of his day', at a time when homosexuality was enjoying something of a vogue. But Douglas did not have affairs with his Oxford contemporaries and coevals; he was for rougher trade. The blackmailing incident over which Wilde had helped him was by no means the first.

But if Wilde was not Alfred Douglas's *beau idéal*, Bosie was certainly his; indeed, Bosie – starting with his nursery nickname itself, so evocative of aristocratic pampering – was everything that Wilde found romantic.

For Wilde all this was the acme of desirability: the conjunction of what was in his eyes physical and physiognomic perfection with sexual voracity was overwhelming. Bosie was witty and clever (though thanks to his chronic laziness, rather ill-read, even if he had read *Dorian Gray*, so he said, thirteen times, which must have made up for a lot).

LORD ALFRED 'BOSIE' DOUGLAS, George Charles Beresford, 1902

Bosie was everything that Wilde was not: young, slim, blond, pale, aristocratic, pampered, perverse. He embodied Wilde's somewhat snobbish vision of aristocracy. The photographic images are again unhelpful in conveying the beauty to which his contemporaries unanimously testified. What to them seemed limpid, in a sort of Quattrocento way, seems to us simply limp; what was then palely loitering, now seems neurasthenic; what was sexy seems simply spent.

They laughed a great deal: Bosie's plaintive objection that Wilde's picture of their relationship in *De Profundis* omitted the laughter that had made up the most part of it rings true. The other side of their life together – and they were together; almost from the moment of their first consummation they became symbiotic despite physical and even emotional separations – the other side, the tempestuous, the terrible, side was the dominant one, on account both of the frequency of its appearance and its virulence when it did.

Bosie was a termagant, a virago, his moods being absolute, enduring no opposition: he wanted what he wanted, when he wanted it, and nothing would stop him from getting it. These spectacular nursery tantrums appalled and thrilled Wilde in equal measure. 'Ouah, il est terrible!' André Gide reports Wilde as saying, admiringly, after one of Bosie's stupendous outbursts at the Café Royal. It was a manifestation, partly of an aristocratic conviction that everything belonged to him as of right, partly of a refusal to be confined or contained. Wilde, for all his suave elegance, was essentially middle class, and knew that he must work for whatever he had; and his professed antinomianism – 'I was born for the exception, not for the rule' – drew the line at hurting other people. Not so Bosie, who might have said, in Aleister Crowley's famous formulation, 'do what thou wilt shall be all the law.'

This trait, which persisted into his embittered and broken old age, had its origins in an unbalanced upbringing, smothered by the love of his mother, denied that of his nearly Neanderthal father, the Marquess of Queensberry, who compensated him with large sums of money with which to divert himself. Interestingly, this pattern was to some extent replicated in his relationship with Wilde: 'I remember very well the sweetness of asking Oscar for the money', Bosie wrote to Robbie Ross, 'It was a sweet humiliation and pleasure for both of us.' Bosie's feelings about his parents were full of contradiction – hysterical loathing of his father, alternating with sudden reconciliations; deep devotion to his mother, allied to a constant need to escape her attentions. The resulting conjunction of guilt and resentment meant that Bosie seemed above all to require Wilde's approval. Unless this was unhesitatingly proffered, hideous splenetic rage – fuelled by feelings of guilt – would ensue. His wrath when Wilde pointed out some of his innumerable schoolboy howlers in his translation of *Salomé* knew no bounds. His attitude to Wilde could be described at the very least as ambivalent. Bosie tormented him with unflattering allusions to his girth and demeanour: when a hotel manager in Algiers had assumed that Wilde was Bosie's father, Bosie delighted in referring to him as *papa*. He demanded Wilde's support and attention, but was often restless in his company. When Wilde failed to be amusing, Douglas was nowhere to be seen.

One of the most sustained examples of Bosie's bad behaviour occurred when he and a boyfriend turned up at Worthing demanding accommodation. Wilde put them up at a local hotel. This was not good enough for Bosie, who, the boyfriend having departed, insisted on being installed in Brighton at the Grand; whereupon he became ill. Wilde came and nursed him, then fell ill himself, at which point Douglas disappeared. He returned, then quarrelled with Wilde and menaced him; Wilde (no physical coward) fled from the hideous emotions unleashed by Bosie. On Wilde's fortieth birthday, Douglas wrote him a letter of violent reproach, ending with the phrase, 'When you are not on your pedestal you are not interesting. The next time you are ill I will go away at once.' So far, so petulant. More complex was his donation of a jacket in whose pocket he had left a bundle of love letters from Wilde to Alfred Wood, a seventeen-year-old he had passed on to Wilde, while continuing to enjoy his favours himself. What, as various biographers have asked, was his motive? It is inconceivable that he simply forgot that the letters were in the jacket. Had he given them to Wood as a way of raising money, the money that he himself was unable or unwilling to give him? Did he intend to put Wilde on the spot? In the event, Wood sent one of the letters to Beerbohm Tree, then about to present *An Ideal Husband*, and attempted to blackmail Wilde, who instead gave him twenty-five pounds to go to America to start a new life. The new life lasted just long enough for him to return to England in time to testify, with damaging effect, at Wilde's trial.

OSCAR WILDE AND LORD ALFRED 'BOSIE' DOUGLAS, Sir Max Beerbohm, n.d.

At an early stage in their relationship Bosie had introduced Wilde to the network of rent boys and working-class pickups that proved, more than anything else, to be Wilde's undoing; increasingly – and without encountering much resistance – he lured Wilde deeper into that world. 'The froth and folly of our life grew often very wearisome to me: it was only in the mire that we met', wrote Wilde in *De Profundis*, 'and fascinating, terribly fascinating though the one topic round which your talk invariably centred was, still at the end it became quite monotonous to me.' Even so he turned it into something marvellous. For Wilde it was a world of mystery and fascination, a forbidden world, fantastic in its dangerous glamour; for Bosie, who seems, in a modern phrase, to have been sexually addicted during his young manhood, it was his drug, the necessary fix. At the end of his life Wilde settled quite comfortably into a louche existence, consorting with street boys, gondoliers and the like, but even then he endowed them with fabulous and no doubt imaginary qualities of personality and sexual prowess, while Bosie in later years felt the need utterly to abjure and indeed deny his former existence.

Wilde claimed that between the sex and the screaming, he was prevented from working, but the list of his literary productions during the period that he knew Bosie gives this the lie. It is certainly true that – despite the continuing excellence of his work – his public personality became increasingly overweening and bombastic, perhaps because there was no still point in his life, no recovery, no refuge. Their life together was always strenuous; from 1893, when Bosie's father first got wind of their relationship, they were to all intents and purposes living under conditions of war. Bosie's response was one of relish for the fray; he delighted in ever greater provocations of his easily roused parent. Oblivious of the dangers – the Labouchere amendment to the Criminal Act, passed in 1885, prescribed severe penal sentences for homosexual offences (just two years before Wilde, with impeccable timing, began his own homosexual career) – Bosie rejoiced in making the issue of his relationship with Wilde a *cause célèbre*, defying both his father and the law of the land simultaneously. He was an active proselytiser of homosexual equality, citing in its favour the work of the German sexologist Krafft-Ebing and the Napoleonic Code, which – prevailing in several European countries – does not include homosexuality as a criminal offence. More importantly he was determined to smash his father for good and all, to punish him for his barbaric treatment of Bosie's mother. In neither of these causes was Wilde particularly interested, but found himself inexorably attached to them.

It was Bosie who urged Wilde to prosecute Queensberry after he had delivered his offensive card to the Albemarle Club; it was Bosie who spurned Frank Harris's advice to Wilde not to proceed with the case ('such advice', he screamed, 'shows you are no friend of Oscar's.' 'That little face blanched with rage and the wild hating eyes, the shrill voice, were Queensberry's', wrote Harris). Bosie begged to be allowed to testify against his father, but Wilde and the lawyers absolutely

Lord Alfred 'Bosie' Douglas, Howard Coster, early 1940s

The *dégringolade* from golden youth to crazed litigant is, for once, all too faithfully reproduced in the photographs, which show the rapid development of the increasingly downwardly turned mouth, the dreamily fanatical eyes, the interrogative nose, a dreadful warning to all ephebes and their admirers: the transformation of Bosie Douglas, Prince Fleur-de-lis, as Wilde once called him, into the croaking frog of Alfred Douglas's mature years. He too was punished, condemned to the living hell of being trapped inside his own personality.

forbade it; his evidence was irrelevant and he was all too likely to become hysterical. When the trial collapsed, it was Bosie who forced him to remain. Having stayed, at some risk to himself, to the bitter end, Bosie went to France; from there he attempted to influence public opinion, even writing to Queen Victoria in terms which can only be described as *de haut en bas* ('In the Hope that your Majesty, remembering that my ancestors have served your ancestors on many fields and in many councils, will not utterly scorn my humble petition'). When Wilde was imprisoned Bosie was refused permission to visit him; he never wrote to him in prison, but persisted in giving interviews about the case until he was stopped by urgent representations from Wilde's friends, in particular Robbie Ross, for whom he began to conceive a deep dislike that flowered twenty years later into a savage vindictive loathing which did as much as anything to send the mild Ross to his early grave.

Meanwhile, meditating in prison on what had brought him there, Wilde had turned against Bosie, and his anger at what their relationship had wrought in his life found its expression in the epic letter that became known as *De Profundis*. When Wilde emerged from gaol, he, Constance, and all his friends made it very clear that he would never see Bosie again. Within months however, they were together, staying in the Villa Giudice in Posilipo, where Wilde finished *The Ballad of Reading Gaol*, his last major work, a work which, Wilde said, was as much about his life with Bosie in Naples as it was about his time in prison. They fought, as before, but bereft of Wilde's glittering public life, and deprived of the drama of defying Queensberry, the excitement of their passionate collision had died, and they parted with some relief, Bosie to an allowance guaranteed him by his mother, Wilde to the desperate rag-picking of his last years. He gave Wilde occasional gifts, but indignantly denied having any further responsibility towards him, as he gambled away fortunes that would have sustained Wilde for the rest of his life. Nonetheless, and despite the continuing deep disapproval of all Wilde's friends, when Wilde died, no one questioned the rightness of Bosie being the chief mourner at the funeral, just as Wilde would have been the chief mourner at his. Bosie paid for the funeral – sixth class.

Bosie's affair with Wilde dominated the rest of his life till the day of his death in 1945. From being a selfish, hysterical and indulgent youth he rapidly graduated in the years after Wilde's death to querulous, embittered, litigious, fanatical, right-wing and religiously obsessed middle-age. Bidding a (fairly lingering) farewell to homosexuality, he married the bisexual poet Olive Custance as early as 1902, having recently converted to Catholicism. They had a son. Then, in 1913, Arthur Ransome's biography of Wilde came out, drawing heavily on information given to him by Robert Ross, in which Douglas emerged as something of the villain of the piece. Douglas took Ransome to court on the matter of libel (how fatal to almost all the participants of the Wilde story that particular offence proved). In defence, the whole of the unpublished sections of *De Profundis*, so profoundly unflattering to Douglas, were read out, and the case collapsed. So, shortly afterwards, did the marriage. Bosie never remarried; his son, increasingly unstable, was confined in a mental hospital as a schizophrenic for the rest of his life. Bosie himself was imprisoned in 1924, having lost yet another libel case – this time against Winston Churchill. His life was now devoted to two themes: establishing his position as a poet, and redefining his relationship to Oscar Wilde, passing in a series of books from a position of outright denial to one of Christian compassion, both for Wilde and for himself. It was a progression of sorts, but not necessarily towards the truth.

It is tempting to see Alfred Douglas as evil, or at the very least criminally selfish. Few people in the history of human relationships have behaved so consistently badly. Yet he was so clearly in the grip of something beyond his control – even at Oxford he had a reputation for not being always responsible for what he said or did – that it is difficult to see him as the conscious author of his actions.

DOWNFALL

THE MARQUESS OF QUEENSBERRY (1844–1900)

John Sholto, 8th Marquess of Queensberry, was one of the most striking of Victorian personalities, as exotic a figure, in his own way, as was Wilde, whose polar opposite he might seem. The collision of these two men was as unlikely as it was spectacular. Had it not been for the accident of Bosie Douglas's liaison with Wilde, it is hard to see how their paths would have crossed. Queensberry, the scion of a long line of suicidal and sometimes sociopathic aristocrats, might have been an averagely hearty sportsman had it not been for the death on a mountainside of his elder brother Francis (followed shortly by the death of his father, leaving him Marquess at the age of fourteen). His brother's death turned him atheist; being who and what he was, he became a militant and highly aggressive atheist, refusing to take the oath of allegiance to God and state ('Christian tomfoolery', he called it), thus denying himself a place in the House of Lords. As a sort of consolation prize, he was invited to become President of the British Secular Society. An early and uncharacteristic encounter with the theatre led to his barracking the First Night of Tennyson's *The Promise of May*, in which the villain was a rakehell and atheist (not unlike several of Queensberry's ancestors, who numbered among them a founder member of the Rakehell Club and an Idiot Cannibal, who after roasting him on the spit ate a kitchen boy). He was meanwhile pursuing his career as a sportsman. Diminutive, he had made himself into an excellent athlete. His equestrian skills were such that he rode his own horses at the Grand National, though to his chagrin he never won it. He was the Amateur Lightweight Boxing Champion of England; indeed, he framed the Rules named after him, which to some extent civilised boxing: his only known contribution to civilisation.

Queensberry's rather eighteenth-century, or perhaps eighteenth-century BC, approach to life continued in the amorous sphere.

Marrying Sybil Montgomery in 1866, he took her to live on his estate in Dumfriesshire; she gave birth to a succession of children (including Alfred, the third child, who was born in 1870) while he took to the hounds, in effect deserting her in favour of his thuggish cronies. He continued his vigorous pursuit of other women despite the dutiful biennial inseminations; these stopped after 1876, with the birth of his daughter Edith. He kept the family on the move from house to house, in search of better hunting. His relations with his children were distant and uncomprehending. His occasional visits to the family home were marked by scenes of violence towards Sybil; from these scenes dated Bosie's hatred of his father. He and his mother grew ever closer, which increased Queensberry's loathing of him and his supposed effeminacy. It was Queensberry who insisted on sending Bosie to Winchester, little realising that he had thrust him into a sexual environment which could only encourage any inclination to homosexuality.

Queensberry seemed to be haunted by fears of sexual deviation. He suspected most of his sons of it (not without reason in the case of two of them). His own emotional life was far from the ideal of Victorian righteousness, however. When he brought his mistress into the house with a view to installing her there permanently, Sybil finally divorced him. His second marriage (to a seventeen-year-old 'of no social standing' – perhaps he and his son had more tastes in common than they imagined) was annulled after six months due to non-consummation, as a result, according to Montgomery Hyde, of Queensberry's genital malformation, impotency and frigidity; quite how he had been able to father his children remains unclear. Though he had managed to get through £400,000 (a prodigious sum for the period) since coming into his inheritance, he never paid alimony until threatened by legal proceedings. He continued to harass his children. When his son Francis inherited the title of Lord Kelhead, he became a member of the House of Lords, a thing denied to Queensberry himself, who wrote in protest to Gladstone and the queen. His rage against the world but especially against his own family simmered volcanically, waiting for an occasion to justify an eruption. He suspected, but was unable to prove, a sexual

JOHN SHOLTO DOUGLAS, 8TH MARQUESS OF QUEENSBERRY
Phil May, 1889

relationship between Francis, by now Viscount Drumlanrig, and the Foreign Secretary, Lord Rosebery, whose private secretary he was. Queensberry threatened to horsewhip Rosebery, but was dissuaded by no less a person than the Prince of Wales; he was balked in his pursuit by the death of Drumlanrig, apparently from a shooting accident, in 1893, impotently railing, 'I smell a Tragedy behind all this and have already *got Wind* of a *more startling one*.' There is something like anguish in the incoherent ravings of a letter in which he denounces 'Snob Queers like Rosebery and Christian hypocrite Gladstone the whole lot *of you*/ Set my son against me indeed and make bad blood between us, may it devil on your own heads that he has gone to his rest and the quarrel not made up between him and myself.' The hapless arrival of Oscar Wilde in his third son's life finally gave Queensberry the occasion he had been waiting for. He was tipped off about the relationship in 1893, and now assumed the unaccustomed role of protective parent and defender of public morals. Bosie instantly smelt the potential of a fight to the death. In fact, what both men loved was the fight itself; the occasion was incidental. It was how they showed their love for each other.

'You are trapped between the tree and the bark', Frank Harris told Wilde; from now on, he was caught in the crossfire which father and son unleashed against each other, only ever hitting the innocent bystander, Wilde. The correspondence between them is a classic of filial and paternal invective: in 1894, Queensberry first wrote to Bosie about 'your intimacy with this man Wilde'. He had seen them together in the Café Royal; had, indeed, joined them at their table, where he had been unexpectedly charmed by Wilde, calming down to the point of apparent rationality. He had swiftly returned to his habitually apoplectic state as soon as he got a pen in his hand. 'With my own eyes I saw you both in the most loathsome and disgusting relationship as expressed by your manner and expression.' He makes, he says, no attempt to analyse 'this intimacy' but 'to my mind to pose as a thing is to be it.' If it *is* true, he says, he will shoot Wilde on sight. Extending the range of his vendettas, he cries, 'These Christian cowards and men, as they call themselves, want waking up.' He signs himself 'your disgusted so-called father'. Bosie replied magnificently, 'What a funny little man you are.' Queensberry now abandoned the pen in favour of personal confrontation, appearing at Wilde's house in Tite Street with a thuggish companion threatening nameless reprisals. 'I don't say you are it, but you look it and you pose it, which is just as bad', he said, indicating a sort of primitive instinct for legal liabilities which was to stand him in good stead. Telling his butler to show the marquess and his thuggish companion to the door – 'this is the most infamous brute in England. You are never to allow him to enter my door again' – Wilde declared that he did not know what the Queensberry Rules were, but that the Oscar Wilde Rule was to shoot on sight. Not to be outdone, Bosie wrote to his father: 'if you try to assault me, I shall defend myself with a loaded revolver, which I always carry' (he did, and one day it went off). The manners of the Wild West had come to town. 'If I shoot you or he shoots you, we shall be completely justified, as we shall be acting in self-defence against a violent and dangerous rough, and I think if you were dead, not many people would miss you.' The idea of Oscar Wilde toting a six-shooter as he glided through his social rounds would be the stuff of high comedy were it not for the context of impending tragedy which increasingly enveloped Wilde.

Nobody was laughing now. Queensberry made it known that he would cause trouble at the First Night of *The Importance of Being Earnest* in February 1895. George Alexander alerted the police and, brandishing his bouquet of carrots and turnips, he was prevented from entering the foyer. While the glow of laughter filled the auditorium, and the heavy snow fell outside, Queensberry stomped round, trying to enter, first the gallery, then the stage door, both of which he was again prevented from doing. The following day, festering with rage, he went to the Albemarle Club of which both he and Wilde were members, leaving a card on which he had almost illegibly scrawled the eccentric phrase 'To Oscar Wilde, posing somdomite [sic]'. The porter placed the card in an envelope which was handed to Wilde on his next visit to the club, some days later. It is to be doubted whether the porter or anyone else would have been able to decipher the intended insult, but for

Wilde, urged on by Bosie, it was the final straw. They determined to prosecute Queensberry for criminal libel, exactly what he had been waiting for. As Wilde and Bosie retreated into a fantasy of victory, stumbling into the case against the advice of all their friends, poorly represented by a legal team which was both inexperienced and naive, approaching palmists and astrologers for omens of success, they took off for Monte Carlo, while Queensberry, driven by a nearly insane determination to smash Wilde and so to save his son, took the practical measures necessary. Hiring teams of private investigators, he uncovered plentiful evidence. Wilde had scarcely been discreet, having been turned out of some of the best hotels in town after being discovered in flagrante delicto. Charles Brookfield, as we have seen, one of the most assiduous informants on the Queensberry side, continued to give his successful performance as the butler Lane in *The Importance of Being Earnest*.

Once the trial began and it soon became clear that Queensberry, represented by the rising legal star Edward Carson, had a vast amount of damning evidence on which to draw, Wilde's case, so jauntily and confidently made when the cross-examination had concentrated on literary matters, collapsed. Queensberry, tasting popularity for the first and only time in his life, was cheered in court. Wilde's letter to the *Evening News* immediately afterwards stated that he had withdrawn from the case because he refused to allow Bosie to take the stand to testify against Queensberry; while Percy Douglas, the eldest surviving brother, publicly denounced his father's 'persecution' of his own family. But Queensberry was now gloriously in the ascendant. He turned over all his evidence to the Crown, which had no option but to proceed with a criminal prosecution. The second trial produced a hung jury; the third was conclusive. During this last trial, Queensberry, who had been crowing triumphantly, shooting off ranting letters and telegrams to Percy Douglas and his wife (accusing Percy, too, of being homosexual), caught a glimpse of Percy in Piccadilly. They met and fought, Queensberry being egged on by a crowd which thought that Percy was Alfred Douglas. 'Queensberry Has A Maul With His Son In Piccadilly', ran the headline. They were bound over to keep the peace, leaving Queensberry free to hasten to the Old Bailey to witness the downfall of his hated foe.

In triumph, Queensberry became almost magnanimous, expressing some sympathy for the fallen man. Or so it was reported. Queensberry wrote to the newspaper in which the story had appeared to define his position a little more clearly: 'Supposing Oscar Wilde was convicted of those loathsome charges brought against him … were I the authority that had to mete out to him his punishment, I would treat him with all possible consideration as a sexual pervert of an utterly diseased mind, and not as a sane criminal. If this is sympathy, Mr Wilde has it from me to that extent.' Once Wilde emerged from prison Queensberry continued his campaign to ensure that he should never be reunited with Bosie, making the by now ritual threat to shoot both of them if they did so; in the event their reunion in Naples passed without the intervention of artillery. In 1899 Queensberry and Bosie had a tender reconciliation, accompanied by a promise of the restoration of Bosie's allowance, but the subsequent condition, that there should be no further dealings with 'that beast Wilde', caused a predictable rift. Queensberry's popularity with the public was short-lived; in a curious parallel to his victim's experience, he found it hard to find a hotel that would accommodate him. He suspected with hilarious misjudgement the influence of 'Oscar Wilders'. His health was breaking down, and he finally expired on 31 January 1900, beating Wilde to the grave by ten months. He managed an extraordinary deathbed scene, telling Bosie's mother that she was his one true love, spitting in Percy's face, and being received into the Catholic Church, again like Wilde, though in Queensberry's case he was apparently fully conscious, making a clean breast of his sins and receiving unconditional absolution.

Alas, Bosie's venomous prediction proved true: not many people missed him, least of all his children. In his book *Without Apology*, written in 1938, Bosie had mellowed somewhat: 'The thought which has recently occurred to me is a terrible one. Did my father really love me all the time, as I certainly loved him before he turned against me, and was he only doing what Oscar says in his great Ballad all men always do, killing the thing he loved? Didn't we all three, Wilde, my father, and I, do it, more or less?'

EDWARD CARSON, 1ST BARON CARSON
(1854–1935)

It is a significant reflection of Wilde's position in society that both Queensberry's counsel were known to him personally: the solicitor, Sir George Lewis, was a member of his family circle, and the barrister, Edward Carson, was a fellow Irishman, a contemporary from Trinity. Lewis had previously acted for Wilde in the matter of Bosie Douglas's blackmailer; he withdrew from the Queensberry case before the action commenced on the grounds of his acquaintance with Wilde. A leading member of the Jewish community and a man shrewd about human behaviour and fully aware of Wilde's sexual history, he told Wilde (who approached him after the collapse of the first trial) that his advice, had it been asked, would have been simply to tear up Queensberry's card and to forget about it. Whether Wilde, with Bosie whispering fiercely in his ear, would have taken such sane advice, is another matter.

Once Wilde discovered that Carson was appearing for Queensberry, he said: 'No doubt he will perform the task with all the added bitterness of an old friend.' It is a significant choice of phrase, the remark of a victim: but Wilde was prosecuting, Queensberry defending. As for their friendship, Ellmann reports that they had known each other as children. Certainly they knew each other at Trinity, where, Wilde said, they used to walk around together, arms draped over each others' shoulders; Carson, naturally, denied this in later life. In any case, they grew apart quickly, Wilde taking the aesthetic, Carson the political, path; both were to become major figures in their respective worlds. Carson was forty-one at the time of the trial, Wilde forty, a fact of which the barrister would make much at an early stage of his cross-examination, the fierceness and brilliance of which has become a legend in legal annals. Wilde, poorly advised by his inexperienced solicitors, and blithe with the confidence of a man who has consulted the oracle and been assured

EDWARD CARSON, 1ST BARON CARSON, Sir Robert Ponsonby Staples, 1898

Wilde and Carson had shared a nanny on a seaside holiday in Dungannon, Co. Waterford. ('Ah,' said Michéal mac Liammóir, 'that would explain it all. Oscar probably upset Edward's sandcastle'.)

of triumph, was under the impression that he had to fight on two fronts: his published writings and his letters to Alfred Douglas. Had this been so, Wilde would have won effortlessly, and Queensberry would have been found guilty as charged of criminal libel; at the discretion of the judge, he could have been imprisoned for up to seven years (as against the two years which Wilde ultimately received). Carson scored a number of skilful points against Wilde – his evasiveness about his age, for example – but in essence he played the straight man, so to speak, to Wilde's elegant clowning, which was much appreciated by the public gallery, who were getting the latest Oscar Wilde play for free.

Several times the increasingly irritated judge had to silence the laughter. Carson (no doubt with perfect sincerity) maintained the stern tone of an outraged moralist, shocked at the wickedness and frivolity of Wilde's aesthetic stance. As long as the subject was art, Wilde managed to make Carson seem clumsy and unsophisticated – this, to a courtroom that was instinctively of Carson's persuasion. It may be that the lawyer's pronounced Irish accent (in sharp contrast to Wilde's velvet vowels) enhanced that impression; he also had a cold as heavy as the accent. Wilde mocked Carson's reading of passages from the letters and books; he pretended not to hear him, or to be deep in distant thought. He even managed to make his extravagant letters to Bosie ('your lips were made for the madness of kissing') seem what he pretended they were, prose poems, intended for publication. The whole Victorian view of life seemed to be under discussion, and Wilde, in witty and perfectly turned phrase after phrase, coolly refuted that view, just as he had done in his plays, to the entire approval, it appeared, of the assembled citizenry.

It was only when Carson shifted the attack to the sexual plane that the thoroughness of Queensberry's work became apparent. The mention of Alfred Wood then ushered in the whole procession of stable boys, waiters, publisher's clerks with whom Wilde had been consorting: the brothers Parker, Fred Atkins, Sidney Mavor. The mood changed decisively. Making witty fun of Victorian values was one thing, crossing the class barrier was another. Up to this point the proceedings had seemed to belong to the boulevard; now they fell into the gutter. Carson pressed his advantage with the utmost ruthlessness. Wilde, flustered, stumbled at the first hurdle. Speaking of Walter Grainger, a servant in Bosie Douglas's house at Oxford, Carson asked whether Wilde had kissed him. 'Oh dear, no,' replied Wilde, fatally, 'he was a peculiarly plain boy. He was, unfortunately, extremely ugly. I pitied him for it.' Carson pressed his advantage, and Wilde, the Lord of Language, the greatest talker of his day, became inarticulate as he tried to backtrack. Finally he said: 'You sting me and insult me and try to unnerve me – and at times one says things flippantly when one ought to speak more seriously. I admit it.' For the first time in public for many years, Oscar Wilde abandoned his pose. He was suddenly intensely vulnerable. 'You have a phrase for everything', Pater had said to him, tartly, at Oxford nearly twenty years before; no longer. After Carson's cross-examination Wilde was examined by his own counsel, Sir Edward Clarke, in an attempt to contain the damage; soon, however, he rested the case for the prosecution. When the court adjourned for lunch Wilde admitted to Clarke that there were matters which could be extremely embarrassing if brought up in court; Clarke, who had secured from Wilde an assurance before accepting the brief that there was no truth whatever in Queensberry's allegations, continued his questioning in the afternoon somewhat shakily.

That afternoon, Carson, vulpine, perfectly focused, took the floor for the defence summing-up, asserting his mastery of the court in a relentless and incontrovertible tirade, indicating the evidence – from Wood, among others – that would be brought, persistently linking Alfred Taylor, the keeper of a male brothel in Little College Street, with 'this man Wilde' (as he had now become). Though Carson explicitly discounted any impropriety between Wilde and Alfred Douglas ('God forbid!') he insisted on the rightness of Queensberry's actions: 'Lord Queensberry was determined to bring the matter to an issue, and what other way was open to him than that which he has chosen?' That night Clarke determined to persuade Wilde to withdraw his prosecution, acknowledging justification of the charge of 'posing' as a sodomite. Before this could happen however, Carson continued in full spate, describing how Wilde had on one occasion dressed a masseur with whom he was having a sexual relationship in the clothes of an English public schoolboy, introducing him in this guise to his wife and son. 'The whole thing in its audacity is almost past belief.' Having painted this comprehensively horrifying picture – a Victorian nightmare – Carson was interrupted by Clarke, who indicated the withdrawal of the case. The jury duly returned a verdict of Not Guilty, and Queensberry was cheered by the court. Carson received a note from the judge, Henn Collins: 'I never heard a more powerful speech or a more searching cross-Xam. I congratulate you on having escaped most of the filth.'

The Crown moved swiftly against Wilde. To Carson's great credit, he immediately approached his friend Sir Frank Lockwood, the Solicitor-General. 'Cannot you let up on the fellow now?' he said. 'He has suffered a great deal.' 'I would,' said Lockwood, 'but we cannot: it would be said at once both in England and abroad that owing to the names mentioned in Queensberry's letters we were forced to abandon it.' So Wilde was tried, not once, but twice: the first time the jury returned a hung verdict, normally indicating a dismissal of the case, but on this occasion a second trial followed swiftly, Lockwood himself led the prosecution. Mr Justice Wills, calling the case 'the worst I have ever tried', imposed the maximum sentence of two years' hard labour – 'in my judgement, it is totally inadequate for such a case as this.'

Carson, it is claimed, passed Wilde after his release from prison in the streets in Paris. After the trial, his eminence as an advocate was triumphantly established; his political career equally proceeded apace. At the time of the trial, he was Conservative MP for Dublin University; he had already been Solicitor-General for Ireland. He occupied the same position in England for six years, from 1900; was Attorney-General in 1915, and First Lord of the Admiralty in 1917, serving in the War Cabinet. Most famously, he founded the Ulster Volunteers, violently opposed to Home Rule for Ireland: 'Ulster will fight, and Ulster will be right!' was his great rallying cry. He occupies a prime position in Ulster's Protestant pantheon; he was first knighted, then made a baron. It is a little ironic, then, as the history of Ireland's troubles recedes, that it should be his involvement in the case of his old schoolfellow Oscar Wilde, whom he must have thought consigned forever to oblivion, that has ensured his immortality.

Frank Harris (1856–1931)

Certain of Wilde's circle came into sharper focus in his life as his fortunes waned. Robbie Ross returned to a central position in his life after playing second or third fiddle to Bosie for some years; and Bernard Shaw and Frank Harris, the latter decisively, became more involved with him around the time of the trial. They were both present, in fact, at what may have been the single most crucial moment in the whole affair. Wilde had asked Frank Harris to testify for him in his libel case against Queensberry as to the literary merit of *Dorian Gray*. Maverick though he was, the diminutive, loud-mouthed Anglo-American had a certain clout as editor of, successively, the *Evening News*, the *Fortnightly Review* and the *Saturday Review*. Born in Wales, he had spent his youth in America, attending the Kansas University; he returned to England, according to Hesketh Pearson, 'with a cowboy's outlook on life tempered by the classics'. Willing though Harris was to testify, he sounded out opinions and concluded that Wilde could never win; over drinks at the Café Royal he urged Wilde to drop the case, with a persuasive and, according to Shaw, uncannily accurate prediction of the probable course of events: 'you haven't a dog's chance – don't commit suicide', he said. 'Don't stay here clutching at straws like testimonials to *Dorian Gray*. *I tell you I know*. I know what is going to happen. I know Clarke's sort. I know what evidence they have got. You must go.' Wilde began to see the force of his argument. It was at this point that Bosie Douglas appeared and denounced Harris with rising and hysterical violence, telling him that his advice proved him to be no friend of Wilde's. Bosie left, after which Wilde, somewhat shakily, echoed the phrase – 'that is not friendly of you, Frank' – and left to pursue the course of action which would lead ineluctably to his destruction.

Now Frank Harris is generally what might be termed an unreliable witness. His preposterously entitled *Oscar Wilde: His Life and Confessions*

FRANK HARRIS, Sir Max Beerbohm, *c.*1911

'Frank Harris has no feelings', wrote Oscar Wilde in the early 1890s, before having proved his sterling worth as a friend. 'It is the secret of his success. Just as the fact that he thinks other people have none is the secret of the failure that lies in wait for him somewhere on the way of Life.'

is a hilariously unconvincing piece of 'faction', and would recall Wilde's remark that 'nowadays every great man has his disciples, and it is always Judas who writes the biography', were it not for the evident good nature of the man who wrote it, and for the fact (one of the few facts to be found in the book) that Harris did know his subject very well, and conveys, through a tissue of invented incident and concocted conversation, a sense of what it was like to be around him. It is also, as Merlin Holland has pointed out, rash to assume that he is *always* unreliable; occasionally, it is Wilde himself who is the fabulist, not Harris. The incident of his advice to Wilde before the first trial is absolutely vouched for by Shaw, who, despite his sometimes suspect judgement in matters personal and political is scrupulously precise with regard to actual events. Harris was a shrewd, good-hearted buffoon, self-serving, but in many ways wonderfully innocent. Between the second and third trials, he invited Wilde, with magnificent insensitivity, to dine at the Café Royal (scene of so many of the encounters that had been and were about to be dissected in court); in the event they went to a restaurant with less associations, and planned Wilde's defence. 'Frank,' Wilde said after a while, 'you talk with passion and conviction, as if I were innocent.' 'Aren't you?' 'No', said Wilde, firmly. 'I thought you knew that.' He then asked Harris if it would make any difference. 'Of course not', replied Harris, and, true to his word, immediately started plotting Wilde's escape, arranging for a yacht to be standing by. Wilde, of course, had no intention of going. During his imprisonment, Harris tried to organise a petition for his early release, but he could persuade no one of any note to sign it.

When Wilde was finally released Harris was ready with an offer of a tour around Europe. Wilde declined: 'It would be a perpetual football match to travel with him.' In 1898 Wilde succumbed to another offer (his financial straits being by now quite desperate) and joined Harris for a trip to La Napoule. Harris claims that they spent their time in vigorous debate over the respective merits of homosexual and heterosexual love. Even though Harris was away for long periods in Monte Carlo, buying a hotel, Wilde was worn out by him: 'Frank insists on my being at high intellectual pressure – it is most exhausting – but when we arrive at La Napoule I am going to break the news to him – now an open secret – that I have softening of the brain – and cannot always be a genius.' He told him, bluntly: 'to survive you one must have a strong brain, an assertive ego, a dynamic character. At your luncheon parties, in old days, the remains of the guests were taken away with the débris of the feast.' Harris took it all in good part. Always trying to encourage him to return to authorship, he offered to write the play of which Wilde had provided the outline for George Alexander, the play about *sheer passion*. He called it *Mr and Mrs Daventry*. It was performed in London in October 1900, produced by and starring Mrs Patrick Campbell (the original Stella Tanqueray, later to create the part of Eliza Doolittle). Wilde's involvement was not publicized, though rumours of his authorship undoubtedly contributed to the financial success it enjoyed despite a largely unfavourable press ('a drama of the dustbin', said Clement Scott). Wilde hoped for royalties, but Harris was obliged to pay off the various other people to whom Wilde had offered advances. This treachery, as he felt it, enraged Wilde. The rage would have passed; instead Wilde did, to a better place, only two months after the opening. Significantly Harris and Bosie were the first people Robbie Ross notified of his death. Wilde's true feelings about the man who had supported him unstintingly in his hours of greatest need are perhaps best expressed in the dedication he wrote to Harris in the printed edition of *An Ideal Husband*: 'A slight tribute to his Power and Distinction as an Artist' – a little poetic licence here, maybe – 'and his chivalry and nobility as a friend' – the simple truth.

GEORGE BERNARD SHAW (1856–1950)

Shaw was quite baffled by the phenomenon of Oscar Wilde, whose complex personality was entirely beyond his ken; but he was in no doubt about his importance as a writer, and his charm as a man. As a young man, he had been a guest at Lady Wilde's *conversazione* in London, but he was of a subtly different social background. Shaw maintained that Wilde was at heart a snob, for which there is plentiful evidence in the superficial sense. He was fascinated by rank, although there was a quixotic element even to this: '*Debrett's Peerage*', he said, 'is the finest thing in fiction done by the English.' On the rare occasions when he chose to put someone down verbally, it would be in terms of their social standing: 'if it had been someone of my own class I might have understood', he said of Beardsley after being stood up for supper. His absolute conviction of the innate superiority of the artist to all other human beings is, no doubt, another form of snobbery. On a deeper level, however, Wilde was profoundly egalitarian, crossing every class boundary and asserting the right of every human being to realise their inherent potential. It was this conviction that led him to attend Shaw's lectures on Fabianism, which in turn provoked his great essay *The Soul of Man Under Socialism*. Wilde had been the only literary man in London to sign Shaw's petition in support of the Chicago anarchists and he was among those Shaw gathered together to promote a new magazine he was about to found. What would it be called, someone wanted to know. 'Shaw, Shaw, Shaw!' cried GBS. 'And how', murmured Wilde, 'will you spell it?'

With the appearance of *Lady Windermere's Fan*, Shaw however became a keen admirer of Wilde as a dramatist, indeed, he sent him a copy of his own first play *Widowers' Houses*: 'I admire the horrible flesh and blood of your creatures', Wilde told him. Thereafter, Shaw wrote with acute appreciation of Wilde's work; he saw the serious purpose

GEORGE BERNARD SHAW, Sir Bernard Partridge, 1894

Wilde clearly regarded the ebullient and earnest compatriot who was none of the things he would ever be – politically committed, asexual and vegetarian – with some affectionate amusement. 'Shaw has no enemies', he averred on one occasion, 'but none of his friends like him.' They did not have a comfortable relationship: 'we put each other out frightfully; and this odd difficulty persisted between us to the very last', said Shaw, 'I was in no way predisposed to like him: he is my fellow-townsman, and a very prime specimen of the sort of fellow-townsman I most loathed: to wit, the Dublin snob.'

behind the surface glitter, viewing the author – no doubt to his surprise and perhaps to his distress – as an essentially Ibsenite dramatist. He saw, too, the skill and the craftsmanship of the work. In his review of *An Ideal Husband*, Shaw says: 'As far as I can ascertain, I am the only person in London who cannot sit down and write an Oscar Wilde play at will.' He was, famously, disappointed by *The Importance of Being Earnest*, the least Ibsenite play, perhaps, ever written; he found that he was not moved by it, and said so in his review, becoming, in effect, the only critic of the original production who failed to hail it as Wilde's masterpiece.

Despite his lack of sympathy with what he called Wilde's perversion ('I have all the normal violent repugnance to homosexuality'), when Wilde was imprisoned, Shaw drafted a petition for clemency, perhaps remembering Wilde's signing of his anarchists' petition; but nothing came of it. Shaw believed that it had made a hero of him: 'for it is the nature of people to worship those who have been made to suffer horribly.' In a comparison that the Wilde of *De Profundis* would surely have relished, he explicitly relates Wilde to Christ: 'if the crucifixion could be proved a myth and Jesus convicted of dying of old age in comfortable circumstances, Christianity would lose ninety-nine per cent of its devotees.' After Wilde's release, Shaw sent him copies of all his books on publication, and received Wilde's in return. Shaw's final verdict on Wilde is odd: believing that Lady Wilde suffered from 'a disease called giantism', he regards him as 'a giant in the pathological sense, and that this explains a great deal of his weakness'. He thought him – as a result of this – incorrigibly lazy. Shaw's final assessment is almost a parody of the man, but there is a kind of ghastly truth in it. 'Oscar seems to have said "I will love nobody: I will be utterly selfish; and I will be not a rascal but a monster; and you shall forgive me everything." In other words, I will reduce your standards to absurdity, not by writing them down, though I could do that so well – in fact, *have* done it – but by actually living them down and dying them down.'

In later life, Shaw became the friend and champion of Alfred Douglas, persuading himself that it was Robbie Ross, not Bosie, who had urged Wilde to prosecute Queensberry, and that history had shamefully misjudged him. He even managed to find Douglas's poetry admirable: 'For this all thy sins be forgiven thee.' It is all part of the quintessential quixotry of a man impelled at all times to side with the underdog, even if he happens to be the son of a marquess.

ADA LEVERSON (1862–1933)

Wife of the merchant Ernest Leverson, the woman Wilde dubbed 'the Sphinx' was a balanced, witty and faithful friend with no ambitions for position within the hierarchy of his friendship, which made her a rarity among Wilde's circle. She saw him clear, from an entirely disinterested angle: 'Oscar is the most generous man I have ever met … he rather resents friends who are not in actual need.' (The instances of Wilde's kindnesses, where he gave of his most precious gift, the full undiluted force of his personality, are legion: on more than one occasion he is credited with having cured toothache by conversation alone.) Mrs Leverson later became an amusing writer – her six novels include *Tenterhooks* and *Love at Second Sight* – and was an admirable correspondent, her sense of fantasy nearly matching Wilde's own: she had, too, an entirely modern ease with his homosexuality. When he had his lover John Gray's slight collection of poems, *Silverpoint*, published in an extravagant edition, she praised the layout: 'the tiniest rivulet of text running through a very large meadow of margin', suggesting that Wilde himself might like to issue a volume which was all margins, 'full of beautiful unwritten thoughts'. Such was the currency of their exchanges, the lightest persiflage. When the iron entered into his soul with the Queensberry affair, she was superbly able to rise to the suddenly greater demands of the friendship. Between the second and third trial, when Wilde was on bail, he had gone, *faute de mieux*, to live with his mother and brother in Oakley Street. Visiting him there, Ada Leverson immediately sensed his unhappiness and invited him to stay with her, an offer he accepted with relief. The only room available to him was the nursery; Mrs Leverson started to move the toys, but Wilde insisted that they remain undisturbed. As described by Ellmann, it was here, solemnly regarded by stuffed animals, that Wilde conducted all the business pertaining to his fast-failing destiny. (Here the young W.B.

ADA LEVERSON
Elliott & Fry, 1890s

ELLIOTT & FRY,   55 & 56, BAKER ST. LONDON. W

Yeats visited him with letters of support from Irish littérateurs. Yeats was among those who was convinced that Wilde had done the right thing by refusing to flee: 'he made the right decision, and to that decision he owes half his renown', an interesting if perhaps arguable position.

That was a minority view among Wilde's friends. Others who came to the Leverson's to persuade him to leave included a tearful

Constance, who in turn persuaded Mrs Leverson to add her weight to the argument. Somewhat reluctantly she did, which disappointed Wilde, who had been happy to pass the time with her as if there were no trial, discussing books and people. 'That is not like you, Sphinx', he said. It was to her that he entrusted his last play, *La Sainte Courtisane*; she was among those who greeted him on his return from prison. She describes the nervousness of the assembled friends as they waited for him. But 'he came in with the dignity of a king returning from exile.' He made a bee-line for her. 'Sphinx, how marvellous of you to know exactly the right hat to wear at seven o'clock in the morning to greet a friend who has been away!' He maintained the banter till the news came that a Roman Catholic retreat to which Wilde had applied would not accept him. Then, at last, he wept. The sun shone again soon after, though, and he continued to receive friends to the point that he missed the morning boat. Then he went off in high spirits, by the boat-train to Newhaven, and thus to Dieppe, under his assumed name of Sebastian Melmoth (a joint allusion to the arrow-slain martyr, a favourite of Wilde's, and the character created by his great uncle Charles Maturin, Melmoth the Wanderer.) He was met off the boat by Robbie Ross and the lawyer Reggie Turner, another good and faithful friend. Somehow he turned this too into an operatic comedy of assumed identities. 'I have thought it better that Robbie should stay here under the name Reginald Turner, and Reggie under the name 'RB Ross', he wrote to Ada Leverson shortly after his arrival. 'It is better that they should not have their own names.' In the same letter, he thanked her for being among the first to greet him. 'When I think that sphinxes are minions of the moon, and that you got up early before dawn, I am filled with wonder and joy … to find you just as wonderful and dear as ever was no surprise. The beautiful are always beautiful.'

He continued his correspondence with Ada Leverson, but they never met again. She was among the many to whom Wilde sent a copy of *The Ballad of Reading Gaol*. Her inscription from him read 'to the Sphinx of Pleasure from the Singer of Pain. Oscar Wilde'.

AFTER THE FALL: FINAL CIRCLE

AFTER THE FALL: FINAL CIRCLE

As he drifted about, ever more dependent on the kindness of strangers, Wilde sang for his supper. Those who bought him a meal or a drink (absinthe for preference) were often rewarded with a story. He told the same tales over and over again, embellishing or simplifying them, as the case might be. Many were versions of stories he had told in his fiction, especially in his *Poems in Prose* from 1894. His gifts as a raconteur, which had dazzled many a glittering audience in the days of his celebrity, now cast a different spell over the more modest gatherings of his last years. The stories he told were often steeped in melancholy, and seemed to make some obliquely paradoxical comment on his own destiny. One such was a distillation of a *Poem in Prose* called *The Master*. 'When Joseph of Arimathea came down in the evening from Mount Calvary, where Jesus had died, he saw seated on a white stone a young man who was weeping. And Joseph went near to him and said, "I understand how great thy grief must be, for certainly that Man was just a Man." But the young man made answer, "Oh, it is not for that that I am weeping. I am weeping because I too have wrought miracles. I also have given sight to the blind; I have healed the palsied and given sight to the blind; I have healed the palsied and I have raised the dead. I, too, have caused the barren fig tree to wither away and I have turned water into wine – and yet they have not crucified me."'

The carnival side of his nature had by no means died, however. He had met Toulouse-Lautrec in London, though he refused to sit for him. One of the most memorable of all the many many images of Oscar Wilde is the pastel portrait of him produced by Toulouse-Lautrec at the time of his trial, where he appears fat, florid, aged and haunted, with the Thames and the House of Commons looming in the background; a lithographic version of this appears in the programme of the Pitöeffs' production – the world première – of *Salomé*. In one of

TOULOUSE-LAUTREC, YVETTE GUILBERT ET OSCAR WILDE
Dans une brasserie proche du Moulin de la Galette, Ricardo Opisso, 1898

Lautrec's many drawings of La Goulue, Wilde's back and quarter-profile are to be glimpsed. There is another image, this time in crayon, not by Lautrec but by Ricardo Opisso, which has great charm: drawn in 1898, it shows Wilde, large and lordly, in the company of Yvette Guilbert and Toulouse-Lautrec himself. Somehow there is a great rightness about this, as if in the Cafés and Music Halls of Paris, seedily glamorous refuge of outsiders, he had found his perfect setting, the sublime fallen joker side by side with the poetess of the sidewalks and the stunted Count who so beautifully painted the underbelly of his city. He looks well and content. There is something Shakespearean about the little tableau: 'you have seen the picture of we three.' Or is it Beckett?

SUGGESTIONS FOR FURTHER READING

Amor, Anne Clark, *Mrs Oscar Wilde: A Woman of Some Importance* (Sidgwick & Jackson, London, 1983)

Borland, Maureen, *Wilde's Devoted Friend: A Life of Robert Ross 1869–1918* (Lennard, Oxford, 1990)

Byrne, Patrick, *The Wildes of Merrion Square* (Staples, London, 1953)

De Vere White, Terence, *The Parents of Oscar Wilde* (Hodder & Stoughton, London, 1967)

Ellmann, Richard, *Oscar Wilde* (Penguin, London, 1987)

Fryer, Jonathan, *André and Oscar: Gide, Wilde and the Gay Art of Living* (Constable, London, 1997)

Gattégno, Jean and Holland, Merlin, *Album Wilde* (Gallimard, NRF, France, 1996)

Goodman, Jonathan, *The Oscar Wilde File* (Allison & Busby, London, 1988)

Harris, Frank, *Oscar Wilde: His Life and Confessions* (The Author, New York, 1916)

Hart-Davis, Rupert (ed.), *The Letters of Oscar Wilde* (Hart-Davis, London, 1962)

— , *More Letters of Oscar Wilde* (Murray, London, 1985)

Holland, Merlin, *The Wilde Album* (Fourth Estate, London, 1997)

Holroyd, Michael, *Bernard Shaw* (Chatto & Windus, London, 1997)

Kingsmill, Hugh, *Frank Harris* (Jonathan Cape, London, 1932)

Montgomery Hyde, H., *Lord Alfred Douglas* (Methuen, London, 1984)

Murray, Douglas, *Bosie: A Biography of Lord Alfred Douglas* (Hodder & Stoughton, London, 2000)

Pearson, Hesketh, *The Life of Oscar Wilde* (Methuen, London, 1946)

Ross, Margery (ed.), *Robert Ross, Friend of Friends* (Jonathan Cape, London, 1952)

Sweetman, David, *Toulouse-Lautrec and the Fin de Siècle* (Hodder & Stoughton, London, 2000)

Wilde, Oscar, *The Collected Works of Oscar Wilde* (Routledge, London, 1994)

Wright, Thomas (ed.), *Tabletalk: Oscar Wilde* (Cassell, London, 2000)

List of Illustrations

© Reproduced by permission of
Merlin Holland

SIR MAX BEERBOHM, 1872–1956
Sir William Nicholson, 1905
Oil on canvas, 50.2 x 40cm
© Estate of Sir William Nicholson
National Portrait Gallery (3850)

AUBREY BEARDSLEY, 1872–98
Frederick Evans, 1894
Platinum print, 14.9 x 10.5cm
© National Portrait Gallery (P115)

SIR HERBERT BEERBOHM TREE, 1852–1917
Harrington Mann, n.d.
Oil on canvas, 68.6 x 57.1cm
© National Portrait Gallery (6197)

GEORGE ALEXANDER, 1858–1918, AS JOHN
WORTHING, WITH ALLAN AYNESWORTH,
1864–1959, AS ALGERNON MONCRIEFFE
In *The Importance of Being Earnest*,
St James's Theatre, 1895
Alfred Ellis, 1895
Cabinet picture, 16.6 x 10.8cm
Theatre Museum © V & A
Picture Library

ROBERT BALDWIN ROSS, 1869–1918
Elliott & Fry, c.1914
Sepia matt print on cream card mount,
15.1 x 20.2cm
© National Portrait Gallery (x12885)

LORD ALFRED 'BOSIE' DOUGLAS, 1870–1945
George Charles Beresford, 1902
Sepia toned platinotype, 15.1 x 10.6cm
© National Portrait Gallery (x28098)

OSCAR WILDE, 1854–1900, AND LORD ALFRED
'BOSIE' DOUGLAS, 1870–1945
Sir Max Beerbohm, n.d.
Pen and ink

© Copyright the Estate of Max Beerbohm,
by permission of London Management

LORD ALFRED 'BOSIE' DOUGLAS, 1870–1945
Howard Coster, early 1940s
Modern print from a 35mm negative,
20.3 x 15.2cm
© National Portrait Gallery (x11389)

JOHN SHOLTO DOUGLAS, 8TH MARQUESS
OF QUEENSBERRY, 1844–1900
Phil May, 1889
Silhouette, 17.8 x 11.4cm
© National Portrait Gallery (3174)

EDWARD CARSON, 1ST BARON CARSON,
1854–1935
Sir Robert Ponsonby Staples, 1898
Chalk, 31.1 x 41.3cm
© National Portrait Gallery (5476)

FRANK HARRIS, 1856–1931
Sir Max Beerbohm, c.1911
Watercolour, 24.8 x 20.3cm
© Copyright the Estate of Max Beerbohm,
by permission of London Management

GEORGE BERNARD SHAW, 1856–1950
Sir Bernard Partridge, 1894
Watercolour, 26.7 x 18.4cm
© National Portrait Gallery (4229)

ADA LEVERSON, 1862–1933
Elliott & Fry, 1890s
Albumen carte-de-visite, 9.3 x 6cm
© National Portrait Gallery (x76184)

TOULOUSE-LAUTREC, YVETTE GUILBERT
ET OSCAR WILDE
Dans une brasserie proche du Moulin
de la Galette
Ricardo Opisso, 1898
Pencil drawing, 39 x 47cm
© Musée de Pontoise, France

CHARACTER SKETCHES
Other titles in the series

Elizabethan Writers
Charles Nicholl

The Romantic Poets and Their Circle
Richard Holmes

First World War Poets
Alan Judd and David Crane

The Bloomsbury Group
Frances Spalding

Dr Johnson, His Club and Other Friends
Jenny Uglow

The Pre-Raphaelites
Jan Marsh

The Irish Literary Movement
A. Norman Jeffares

Soho in the Fifties and Sixties
Jonathan Fryer

Tennyson and His Circle
Lynne Truss

Fitzrovia: London's Bohemia
Michael Bakewell

Samuel Pepys and His Circle
Richard Ollard

*Winner of the 1998 Gulbenkian Award for
Best Museum Publication*